GW00320305

We are like Dreamers

by Walter Beyerlin

WE ARE LIKE DREAMERS
Studies in Psalm 126

by WALTER BEYERLIN
Translated by Dinah Livingstone

T. & T. CLARK LIMITED, 36 GEORGE STREET,
EDINBURGH

First published in Great Britain 1982, by
T. & T. Clark Limited, 36 George Street,
Edinburgh EH2 2LQ, (Tel: 031-225-4703).

Published in Germany by
Verlag Katholisches Bibelwerk, Stuttgart, 1977

ISBN: 0 567 09315 8

Printed in Great Britain by
William Blackwood & Sons Ltd
162 Leith Walk, Edinburgh EH6 5DX

Contents

Dedicated to Uta and Wilhelm Rudolph

Introduction

Psalm 126 is one of the outstanding texts in the psalter. In form and content it is a little masterpiece. Its words go straight to the heart and are unforgettable: 'When the Lord restored the fortunes of Zion . . . then our mouth was filled with laughter, and our tongue with shouts of joy' and 'He that goes forth weeping, bearing the seed for sowing, shall come home with shouts of joy . . .' These two quotations alone give us an idea of the psalm's quality. Commentators recognise this quality and describe it as superlative. An example is the impressive praise with which Bernhard Duhm ends his commentary: 'One of the most beautiful poems, perhaps the most beautiful in the whole psalter, both in content and form. Nowhere else is the eschatalogical hope expressed with such heartfelt, touching simplicity, there is no other poem which expresses this deep and beautiful thought . . . by such simple means, nowhere else does this longing come so humanly close, even to the non-Israelite, as it does here.'(1)

But in spite of the high quality generally ascribed to the psalm, we have the problem that in nearly all the questions upon which its interpretation depends, opinions are sharply divided. This is no less true of recent research than of earlier commentaries. (2)

The trouble is a group of problems inherent to the poem which are difficult to come to grips with. One of these problems, which I think makes the interpretation of the psalm particularly difficult, is not even recognised as a problem by many scholars. (3)

Thus we have a psalm poem of high quality, which is also difficult to understand and its problems by no means solved, which means that it is unquestionably worth the effort of further investigation. We must begin by pointing out the problems which cause difficulties in understanding the psalm.

---

[1] KHC XIV, 437. In references to (Psalm) commentaries book titles are omitted.

[2] Cf. with B. Duhm op.cit. 436f, e.g. H.-J. Kraus, BK XV/2, 853-57; A. Weiser, ATD 14/15, 524-526; M.Dahood, AncB 17A 217-221 or also A.A. Anderson, NCeB, 863-866.

[3] See below Chap. 1.6.

1. The Problems in detail

1.1 Our psalm appears to have a contradiction in it. In the first part, verse 1-3 (4) the restoration of Zion (5) is presented as already accomplished. The community expressing itself in prayer with the psalms proclaims: 'The Lord has done great things for us; we are glad.' (V.3.) Then the tone changes. Restoration is prayed for(!), and thus clearly in the future: 'Restore our fortunes, O Lord, like the water courses in the Negeb!' (V.4.) Then the text goes on to recognise that there is still weeping and that we live in suffering and want (VV. 5.6.). Thus we have a psalm in two contradictory parts! 'Two distinct and contrasting moments; two opposite states of mind'! (6)

Commentators take it as certain that the two parts refer to different times. How else can the contradiction be resolved? It is also commonly accepted that Part II, verses 4-6 refer to our present condition. (7) But then agreement comes to an end. The dispute continues even now as to *how* a time difference between the two parts of the psalm could come about. Some commentators (8) regard Part I as referring to experiences of the past, while others (9) argue the contrary: Part I does not look to the past but

---

[4] Not counting the editorial title 'A Song of Ascents'.

[5] For the textual rendering c.f. Chap. 4.1.

[6] G.R. Castellino, 842.

[7] Except for M. Dahood, op.cit. 218.220. We say more about this exception later.

[8] J. Ohlshausen, KEH, 457; W.M.L. de Wette, 548; H. Hupfeld, vol. 4, 285; F. Baethgen, HK II 2, 381; W. Staerk, SAT Part 3, vol, 122f; R. Kittel KAT XIII, 396; H. Schmidt, HAT 115, 226f; H. Herkenne, HSAT V 2, 407; E.A Leslie, 126f; F. Nötscher, EB, 277f; H.-J Kraus, op. cit, 854; E.J. Kissane, 578; J. J. Weber, 548f; C.C. Keet, *A Study,* 49f; A.A. Anderson, op. cit., 863, among others.

[9] B. Duhm, op. cit, 436; A. Bertholet, HSAT, (K) vol. 2, 258; H. Gunkel, HK 2, 551; M. Buttenwieser, LBS, 281ff; W.O.E. Oesterley, 515; A. Weiser, op. cit., 524f., among others.

to the future. (10) An apparently irreconcilable difference of opinion! It brings out a crucial problem that must be reconsidered.

1.2 This same problem also causes grammatical difficulties. What is the tense of the verbs in Part I? Various answers are given to this question. On the one hand there are those who hold that the perfect used to refer to the future 'is impossible'. (11) The perfect verses 1 and 3 can *only* refer to the past. The imperfect in verse 2 goes together with these perfects and refers to the same time, viz. the past. And there is no doubt that the infinitive $(b^{evn}su\dot{b})$ in verse 1 must also have a past reference. (12) On the other hand, other scholars dispute the grammatical necessity for these assumptions. Those who make them show 'a defective knowledge of the language'. (13)

The perfect in verse 1 refers to 'blessed future moment when happiness is suddenly attained' (14) The perfect in verse 3a must be taken as a prophetic perfect. (15) But even when this part of the psalm is not making a prophetic proclamataion, but is a meditation reaching into the future, the perfects in verses 1 and 3 still refer to future events (16) as do the other verb forms. On reflection this difference of opinion is not surprising. Hebrew verb syntax is always a problem. Hebrew does not have tenses in the

---

[10] Weiser tries to mitigate the either-or: The hope which as such is future directed, also refers back to 'earlier experiences of divine intervention from the cultic tradition'. op. cit. 524.

[11] See H. Schmidt, op.cit., 226

[12] See F. Baethgen, op.cit., 381, appears to mean this and others.

[13] B. Duhm, op.cit., 436.

[14] Ibid., op.cit.

[15] See H. Gunkel, op.cit., 551.

[16] Cf. D. Michel, *Tempora und Satzstellungen,* 243.

sense of verb forms designating past, present or future time. (17) The time reference must be derived from the context. (18) The verb forms in the psalm text do not help to solve the problem of how the two contradictory parts of the psalm can be differentiated, by time or otherwise. (19) The grammatical difficulties simply bring us slap up against the problem!

1.3 There is also disagreement about the psalm's literary form. If Part I refers to the past, then Psalm 126 may seem to be a People's Lament. (20) Looking back to a happier past is commonly held to be characteristic of a People's Lament. (21) On the other hand, when Part I is taken to be 'in the style of prophecy' (22) and therefore referring to the future, the literary form is described as 'prophetic liturgy', in which prophetic oracle and people's lament go together'. (23) This means a liturgy created for use in the divine service, which should keep the prophetic message of salvation alive. (24) At this point opinions differ even further.

---

[17] See for example, R. Meyer, Hebräische Grammatik, III 39.   The verb has not *tenses* strictly speaking. It has two forms, which express not time but the quality of an action as complete or incomplete; the one expresses a finished action, and is called the *perfect,* the other an unfinished action and is called the *imperfect.*' A.B. Davidson, *Introductory Hebrew Grammar* (Edinburgh, 1960 edition), 20.2., p.72.

[18] *Ibid.,* op.cit. 42.49.

[19] The imperative in verse 4 gives an important clue, but it is not sufficent on its own.

[20] See H. Schmidt, op.cit 226. See also E. J. Kissane, op.cit., 578, who calls it a community prayer of petition, as does J. J. Weber, op.cit., 548. A. A. Anderson (op.cit., 863f) discusses and deliberates on the problem without coming to any clear conclusion, which makes it difficult to place him.

[21] See the enumeration of elements specific to literary forms in H. - J. Kraus, op.cit., 551.

[22] H. Gunkel, op.cit., 551.

[23] *Ibid.,* op.cit.

[24] Cf. H. Gunkel - J. Begrich, *Einleitung* para 4 (14) 138 a, d; para. 11 (20) 414.

Quite a number of commentators hold that there is an additional sharp break between verse 4 and what follows. Verse 4 prays for the restoration of Zion. Verses 5 and 6 contain corresponding words of comfort: 'He that goes forth weeping, bearing the seed for sowing, shall come home with shouts of joy . . .' Those who take this view of a sharp break after verse 4 may still disagree in their evaluation of it. Some hold that verses 5 and 6 are 'comforting thoughts' suited to a People's Lament (25) and therefore not a reason against the asssignment of the poem to this literary form. (26) Others take a different view, that rather than in Part I, it is here in the closing verses that we have a separate oracle, which should be distinguished from the People's Lament. (27) Then the connection between this separate oracle and what precedes it is also disputed. The connection is either genuine liturgy; the prayer of the community is given a prophetic or perhaps even priestly response. (28) Or the connection of the two parts is a poetic imitation based on the model of the liturgy. (29) Recently the range of form-critical opinion has become even wider. (30) It includes the amazing idea that Psalm 126 is a hymn. (31) This is based on a bold philological hypothesis: In verse 4 where the Masoretic text has an imperative request, the original

---

[25] H. Gunkel op.cit., 552; H. Gunkel - J. Begrich op.cit., para 4 (10) 131. Others who agree with Gunkel here are: H. Schmidt op.cit; E. J. Kissane op.cit.; A. A. Anderson op.cit. and others.

[26] H.-J. Kraus (op.cit. 854-6) also agrees with the possibility of this interpretation.

[27] See E. A. Leslie, op.cit, 126f and A. Weiser, op.cit., 525, E. Bauman, *Struktur-Untersuchungen* (115-152) 144, and possibly also Kraus, op.cit.

[28] See A. Weiser, op.cit., also, apparently E. Baumann op.cit. and S. Mowinckel, *The Psalms,* II, 76.

[29] This, if I have understood him right, is the view of E. Leslie, op.cit., 127.

[30] For what follows cf. M. Dahood, op.cit., 217-220.

[31] 'A hymn of thanksgiving', op.cit., 217.

form was a perfect, an archaic form of the perfect (32) possibly a Phoenician derived consonantal transcription and pronunciation. (33) In this case verse 4 does not pray for restoration, the restoration of the Lord's community, but looks back on it as a *fait accompli*, using the perfect form. This means that Part II, like Part I, refers to an earlier state of salvation. Thus the tension in the Masoretic text is resolved in satisfaction. Looked at in this way, the Psalm is a hymn throughout. It is philologically homogenous, but by means of assumptions which are more difficult to accept than the tensions in the Hebrew text come down to us, that they seek to resolve. (34) Is it a hymn or people's lament? An ordinary lament or liturgy? An oracle at the beginning or the end of the text? Liturgical speech or a poetic imitation? The answer appears to be: *'Quot homines, tot sententiae!'*

1.4. Even the question of its historical context is not settled. Here the difference of opinion is reflected less clearly. For conclusions about its form only occasionally result in ensuing conclusions about its context. If the Psalm is regarded as a hymn then of course its context must be a festival of the Lord. (35) If it is seen as a liturgy, artistically sensitive late liturgy, (36) the only thing that can be said definitely about it is that it found a place in the

---

[32] Saba instead of the imperative Sûba

[33] Sôba

[34] The Psalm does not derive from the early period (see below Chap. 4.1. - 4.5.). So how can it contain numerous archaic forms? Or a Phoenician derived diction and writing?

[35] . . . composed for one of the religious festivals', M. Dahood, op.cit. 217.

[36] Not the well-known succession of people's lament and answering oracle of salvation which would allow it to be referred back to the Fast Day *(Sôm)*. Cf. also H. Gunkel - J. Begrich op.cit. para. 4 (2) 117ff; para. 11 (15) 410f. For the liturgy of the later stages cr. Gunkel-Begrich op.cit. para. 11 (20.21) 414f. Like all the other commentators who take it as a liturgy, they appear to mean a late new version. Clearly so does A. Weiser op.cit., 524

cult. (37) If it is regarded as a liturgical-sounding poem, of course we can come to no conclusions about where it was recited. If it is taken as a people's lament, we can only draw one conclusion: that it was meant for a fast day. That it was not in fact used for this (38) is distinctly curious (39) but is partly in spite of the different forms by which it is categorised, attempts to place it in a historical context seems to converge. When anything relevant is said, (40) it is related in general to the cult, or with a bit more precision to the festival liturgy. Particular hypotheses that it was connected with this or that liturgical festival (41) are not well enough supported by the text and only serve to reveal how many questions remain unanswered.

1.5 There is agreement on one thing about its historical placement: Psalm 126 must be dated as post-exilic. If its introductory part is related to the *past,* to salvation once experienced, (42) this still means that it is thinking about the exiles' triumphant return from exile in Babylon. (43) It follows

---

[37] Here too see Gunkel-Begrich op.cit. para. 11 (21), 414f and R. Kittel op.cit., 395 The latter only makes cautious suggestions. Likewise J.J. Weber op.cit., 548 *('. . . chantées sans doute par deux choeurs . . .').*

[38] Cf. especially H. Schmidt, op.cit., 226f.

[39] Is this merely the narrowness of the HAT commentary? Schmidt's view leads to the supposition but not proof that a practical historical context is not envisaged.

[40] And in psalm commentaries from Gunkel on, this is not always the case!

[41] New Year, Harvest or Tabernacles. Cf. E.A. Leslie, op.cit., 126; A. Weiser, op.cit., 524; A.A. Anderson, op.cit.,864.

[42] See above 1.1., especially note 8.

[43] Cf. J. Ohlshausen, op.cit., 457; W. M. L. de Wette, op.cit., 584- H. Hupfeld, op.cit., 285- F. Baethgen, op.cit., 227-; H. Herkenne, op.cit., 407; F. Nötscher, op.cit., 277; H.-J. Kraus, op.cit., 854f- E. J. Kissane, op.cit., 854f- E. J. Kissane, op.cit., 578; G. R. Castellino, op. cit., 842 ; J.J. Weber, op.cit., 548 and (perhaps!) A. A. Anderson op.cit., 864. (Exceptions are E. A. Leslie, op.cit., 126f and A. Weiser, op.cit., 524).

that our psalm's terminus *post quem* is 538B.C.. On the other hand, to elucidate the second half of the text as well, with its prayer for help (v.4) we must posit a later period, a period of disillusionment and disappointment. Commentators assess this very differently. Some hold that the psalm dates from 'a few years after the return' (44) in the dark days of the prophet Haggai (45), or as contemporary with the Third Isaiah. (46) Others date this prayer for help later, according to one, not until the time of Esra and Nehemiah (mid 5th centuryB.C.), (47) and according to another the year 400 at the earliest, (48) according to a third, not until the Hellenic period, (49) perhaps in the context of the revolt of the Maccabees (mid 2nd century B.C.). (50) This survey shows how difficult it is to be definite. Attempts to date it waver through the centuries of the post-exilic era. But things are no easier when the first half of the psalms is related to the *future*. (51) Seen thus it is a song of eschatological hope ascribed to 'Judaism' (52) or, as it is otherwise called, the small post-exilic nation. (53)

---

[44] H. Schmidt expressly, op.cit. Others by implication.

[45] Hag. 2.16 and 1.6, 10,11 are quoted here with various interpretations. Cf. H. Schmidt, op.cit; H.-J. Kraus, op.cit., 855; J. J. Weber, op.cit; R. Kittel, op.cit.

[46] Cf. especially H. -J. Kraus, op.cit. We should note by the way that it is barely possible to establish the chronology here.

[47] Thus A. F. Kirkpatrick.

[48] J. Morgenstern, *Psalm 126*, 114f.

[49] C.A. and E.G. Briggs ICC, vol. 2, 456. This commentary also holds that the psalm's introduction is a 'general statement'. Even understood thus, this half of the text is related to experiences undergone, and hence to the past.

[50] Thus J. Ohlshausen, op.cit., 457.

[51] See also chap. 1.1., note 9.

[52] Thus H. Gunkel, op.cit., 552.

[53] Thus B. Duhm. op.cit., 437.

Once again this placing shows how difficult it is to determine the poem's historical context. And this raises the question again of whether the preference for a post-exilic date can really be justified. Its closeness in thought to the prophecy of Deutero-Isaiah leads some to date it during the exile. (54) On the other hand its linguistic archaisms (or what are seen as archaisms!) make some venture to suggest that the psalm might be even earlier. (55) Others do not even attempt to date it. (56) All in all it is clear that even the question of the age and date of our poem is by no means settled and needs to be reconsidered.

1.6 Of course the themes of the psalm also cause problems. (57) This is certainly the case with the half verse 1.b. Understanding of the text as a whole is surprisingly dependent on this sentence: 'we are (or were/will be) (58) like those who dream *(hajînû keholemîm).*'

Some commentators do not have a word to say about this expression, as if it were self-explanatory. (59) Others hurry past with a deft paraphrase. (60) Others again explain it in a roundabout way: The comparison with dreamers means that they took what was reality 'for a dream', (61) for a 'beautiful dream',

---

[54] Cf. M. Buttenwieser, op.cit., 281ff, 285ff.

[55] Cf. M. Dahood, op.cit., 217f.

[56] This is especially the case when the presumption is that the text was repeatedly recited liturgically through the ages: Cf. E. A. Leslie, op.cit., 126-8 and A. Weiser, op.cit., 524-6.

[57] This is hardly true any longer of sûb sebût/sûb 'at-sîbat (v.4 and v.1). See no. 4.1

[58] For the problem of tenses, here excluded, see above, chap. 1.2. and below chap 3.3.

[59] Cf. R. Kittel, op.cit., (At any rate the translation given enables us to draw rough conclusions).

[60] Cf. B. Bonkamp, op.cit. p. 552 or J.J. Weber op.cit., p. 548.

[61] W.M.L. de Wette, op.cit., p. 585.

(62) or, significantly, 'only' a dream (63) — which means a 'self deception . . . such as we get from a dream when we are asleep'. (64) This means that we have made a mistake and must change our thinking. For the salvation dismissed as a 'dream' or self-deception, was strange and wonderful but still real. At any rate — so the argument continues looking at the second half of the psalm — this reality, however wonderful it might be, did not afterwards satisfy, it was even a disappointment. (65) The straight 'we are like those who dream' becomes a thought spiral. Not just simply: we *are* like those who dream' but 'we think we are'. (66) Or even: 'we wrongly think we are but in fact are not, we are not subject, as we thought at first, to self-deception, but see things as they are; we find it difficult to grasp them because they are so strange.' (67) And, the marvel of this salvation which is almost incomprehensible still leaves something to be desired! This explanation is a bit too complicated!

Odd though it is, many commentators adopt this view, which of course does not dominate the field. Before, beside, and after it there are other attempts at interpretation. There is the view that the comparison with dreamers means: We are amazed at God's

---

[62] Cf. F. Baethgen, op.cit., 381, W. Staerk, op.cit., 122; F. Nötscher, op.cit., 277f and also E.L. Ehrlich, *Der Traum in Alten Testament,* 154.

[63] Thus H. Herkenne, op,cit., 407.

[64] Jacob and Wilhelm 'Grimm's *German Dictionary,* vol. 11, section I, part 1, 1450.

[65] The following argue thus: H. Hupfeld, op.cit., 286; F. Baethgen, op.cit.; W. Staerk, op.cit., 122f; B. Duhm, op.cit., 436f; H. Schmidt, op.cit., 227; H.-J. Kraus, op.cit., 855-57; and apparently also A.A. Anderson, op.cit., 864f.

[66] Hupfeld makes a distinction here — quite wrongly in my view — and interprets it as 'futile', op.cit.

[67] '... it was like a dream ... unbelievable!' E. Routley, *Exploring the Psalms, 87.*

marvellous power. (68) There is also the view that the comparison is a manner of speech: 'We would hardly have allowed ourselves even to dream this'; (69) in this case 'dream' means phantasise or imagine. (70) Or 'being like dreamers' is an expression for being elated or entranced. (71) Zion felt 'almost' as if it were changing into a dream. (72) Or the comparison is used for an ecstatic state: Those who compare themselves to dreamers are in an ecstasy of joy. (73) It also suggested that the dream in question was a charismatic-prophetic dream: The speakers here compared themselves to charismatics, people who were full of laughter and joy through the outpouring of the divine Spirit. (74) On the other hand, it was also compared to the bad dream and its fleeting quality. To be like dreamers means like people who have a bad dream, which they then quickly forget. (75) Enough said! (76) What contradictory interpretations! And nearly all of them claim to be proven and obvious. (77) This summary of interpretations shows how glaring the problem is. Where there is confusion, even

---

[68] Thus A. Weiser, op.cit. 525.

[69] Cf. F. Nötscher, op.cit. 277.

[70] Cf. *German Dictionary* 1490.

[71] 'Here the dream is an image for a particularly elated mood.' A. Resch, *Der Traum im Heilsplan Gottes,* 50.

[72] Thus E. A. Leslie, op.cit. 127.

[73] C.A. and E.G. Briggs, op.cit. 456; fundamentally the same also Hengstenberg (following Hupfeld, op.cit.); more recently, very much the same, C.C. Keet, op.cit., 50 ('... dazed by joy').

[74] Thus W.O.E. Oesterley, op.cit., 515f.

[75] Basically, *Qimhi* (according to C.C. Keet, op.cit.); cf. also J. Ohlshausen, op.cit. 458.

[76] Although the problem is not settled. Cf. in particular A. Wünsche, *Midrasch Tehillim,* 208.

[77] W.O.E. Oesterley and A.A. Anderson are exceptions among the psalm commentators. On the other hand cf. e.g., C.C. Keet: op.cit.: '... the usual meaning, viz., that they were dazed by joy ...'

if the individual commentator is unaware of it, we have a *crux interpretum*. When interpretations clash, (78) the trouble may be that we are not clear about many different ways we speak about dreaming in our own language. (79) Perhaps the first thing necessary is to look in Jacob and Wilhelm Grimm's *German Dictionary*. (80) One thing remains to be said: Although, as we saw, nearly all modern commentators. (81) are unaware of the difficulty of this half verse, (1b) we should note that the ancients, in various ways, clearly were aware of it. The scribe to whom we owe the psalm manuscript from the 11th Qumran Cave (11 QPs.a), apparently avoided by far the most common rendering. He understood the Hebrew expression (82) as passive, in the sense of being healed, being restored to health ('... like those who are healed / or: who have been healed'). (83) Some of the versions have done likewise. For example the Septuagint (84) and following it, the Psalterium Gallicanum. Both translate as 'like those who are comforted'. The Peshitta reads '.... like those who rejoice'. The Qumran attempt to render the phrase 'healed/strengthened' has occasionally found support in recent times; (85) the typical reason given for this is that in the context of the psalm

---

[78] Cf., as an example F. Nötscher, op.cit. 277-8.

[79] The author is writing in German but adds the footnote: This is also true of other modern languages, including English.

[80] A glance into the *Oxford English Dictionary* / vol. 3, 655ff. will show that this also affects English-speaking commentators. Here I would like to thank two Münster colleagues, H. Kruse, Professor of English and F. Ohly, professor of German who helped me study these dictionaries.

[81] See above note 77.

[82] With the help of the *mater lectionis* w in *khlwmjm*.

[83] Cf. J.A. Sanders, *The Psalm Scroll of Qumran Cave 11,* 25 and A.A. Anderson, op.cit. 864.

[84] Perhaps on the basis of a Hebrew original such as we have in 11 QPs, a.

[85] J. Strugnell, *A Note on Ps, CXXVI. 1,* 239-243. M. Mannati Vol. 4, 152, also supports this rendering and even translates as: '... *comme des ressuscités!*'.

this is the only rendering that will do, which 'dreaming' will not. (86) It is worth noting that one of the most recent psalm commentators simply deletes the Hebrew word for 'dreaming' (as a textual error!) and offers as his reason that no one has ever succeeded in making sense of the comparison with dreamers in the context. (87) I do not think it is right to change the Masoretic text (88) or to evade the interpretation 'like dreamers' (89) But I do think it is important to realise that up till now this comparison has not been satisfactorily explained. And as long as this is so, it seriously hinders the understanding of the psalm as a whole. We therefore want to discuss the meaning of verse 1b further.

---

[86] J. Strugnell, op.cit. 242f.

[87] M. Dahood, op.cit. 218-9.

[88] This by the way I hold not only for Psalm 126 but elsewhere.

[89] *hlm*, as the concordances show, means 'dream' in the overwhelming majority of cases.

2. The Comparison with Dreamers

In the Babylonian Talmud in the Tacanit treatise, folio 23a, we hear of Honi the drawer of circles: 'Every day of his life this good man fretted about this verse.' (1) Here the meaning is this verse of our psalm, and especially this comparison. What must we do so as not to spend longer than necessary, certainly not as long as our good man, fretting over this text?

2.1 First we must ask what ways of speaking about dreaming and dreams were *not* available to the ancient Israelite poet, (2) which of the various interpretations we found in our commentators presuppose later meanings derived from the development of the German (or English) language. Such usages could hardly have been current in biblical Hebrew two thousand years earlier. In our efforts to understand Psalm 126 v. 1b they must be set aside as linguistic modernisms. With this in mind let us take a look at Jacob and Wilhelm Grimm's German Dictionary. We find the following: 'Its original reference was to the sleeping state .. all meanings which do not presuppose a sleeping condition only came into use in later and recent stages of language.' (3) This immediately dismisses some of the interpretations mentioned above. For example the rendering: 'We could scarcely have dreamt this.' This interpretation does not refer to sleep and a dream during sleep, but a waking dream and continues with 'we could scarcely believe it possible' or 'we would hardly dare to

---

[1] L. Goldschmidt, *Der babylonische Talmud, vol. 3, p. 715;* A. Wünsche, *Midrasch Tehillim II,* p. 208.

[2] As this question has not been considered by commentators, we are justified in stressing its importance at the beginning of our discussion. For generations its neglect has hampered the exegesis of the psalm. Clearly only research on how Old Testament Hebrew speaks of dreaming and dreams can be finally decisive,

[3] op.cit. 1437; cf. also 1450 and 1478.

hope it' and comes from a late stage in the language. (4)

'Amazement' is also remote from the sleeping condition and can only be connected, if at all (which is doubtful) with a waking dream. This is also an association which only became possible in a highly developed late stage of the language. But also the reading that being like those who dream means fear, irrational fear, which is then found to be unreal, refers to a waking dream and derives — anachronistically — from a late stage of the German language. (5) Likewise the interpretation that the comparison with dreaming means that Zion almost felt that it was going about in a dream. This comparative way of speaking about a dream, especially when it expresses the feeling of being 'spirited away from present reality' (6) was only possible in educated speech from the Middle High German period and only became widespread after the Romantic period. (7) This is another example of how wrong it is to try to interpret our ancient Israelite psalm verse by means of later usages of 'dream' and 'dreaming'. Briefly, it is clear that quite a number of the interpretations we have mentioned depend on linguistic modernisms and are therefore invalid. Put simply, the nature of the development of the German — and English — language (8) leads us to expect that only those attempts at interpretation can be seriously considered, which interpret the comparison with dreamers, as dreamers in sleep.

---

[4] Cf. *German Dictionary*, 1494f.

[5] Cf. *German Dictionary*, 1450f. The Romantic A. von Arnim could say 'he thought ... everything he had experienced had been only a dream'; A. von Droste-Hülshoff could write: 'whether it was a dream or reality was questionable here'. How could this way of speaking about dreams be available to the ancient Israelite poet? For 'dream image' see also, *German Dictionary*, 1474f.

[6] *German Dictionary*, 1449f.

[7] Ibid., 1447-1449f. See also *The Oxford English Dictionary*, 655 (4c).

[8] *The Oxford English Dictionary*, 655f.

2.2 This impression gained from the facts obtained within the German (and English) language, needs counter-proof (9) from within the Old Testament. How are dreams and dreaming spoken of in biblical Hebrew? (In our treatment of this question, we depend chiefly for support from Ernst Ludwig Ehrlich's book *Der Traum im Alten Testament,* 1953). (10) and then on A. Leo Oppenheim's study, 'The Interpretation of Dreams in the Ancient Near East,' 1956. (11) One thing is clear — in none of the relevant texts does 'dreaming' or 'dream' mean any kind of waking dream. Of course sleep is not always expressly mentioned. But in all cases it is assumed. Where there is no sleep there is no dream. (12) Let us give some examples. Jacob awakes from sleep after he has dreamt at Bethel (Gen. 28.16). (13) God comes to Abimelech 'in a dream at night' (Gen. 20.3), and also to Laban at night (Gen. 31.24); '... Solomon awoke and lo, it was a dream' (1 Kings 3.15). Job is depressed by dreams in bed, dreams while he sleeps (Job 7.13,14). The dream in which God reveals himself happens (usually) at night, and if not when they are asleep 'when they slumber on their beds' (Job 33.15,16). (14) Even when a dream is used as a comparison for transitoriness, nothingness, self-deception, it is unquestionably a sleeping dream and not a waking dream: 'And the multitude of all the nations ... shall be like a

---

[9] *Sit venia verbo!* See above note 2.

[10] BZAW, 73. See also Ehrlich, *Traum,* BHH III, 2023-2025, and also A. Resch, *op cit.*

[11] In: *Transactions of the American Philosophical Society,* NS vol. 46, part 3, 1 7 9 - 3 7 3 .

[12] Sleep is a necessary condition for dreaming. Cf Ehrlich, BZAW, 145 and the definition of a dream in BHH III, 2023: 'Dream ... an experience during sleep ...'. When sleep is not expressly mentioned, it can always be inferred. For example, see Ehrlich, BZAW, 58ff., 85ff.

[13] This is true whatever the literary critical judgement of the passage. Cf. Ehrlich, BZAW, 27f.

[14] For an analysis of this passage see G. Fohrer, KAT XVI, 453, 454 (458).

dream, a vision of the night. As when a hungry man dreams he is
eating, and awakes with his hunger not satisfied, or as when a
thirsty man dreams he is drinking and awakes faint, with his thirst
not quenched, so shall the multitude of all the nations be ...' (Is.
29.7,8).(15) The transitoriness and unreality of what is dreamed in
sleep is the *tertium comparationis*. The comparison in Psalm 73.20
applied to the godless is also with a dream in sleep. The 'despising
when you awake' leaves no doubt about it. Even when the dream
is a literary device (as in Daniel Chapters 2 and 4) dreams dreamt
in sleep are meant. Thus whether the dreams are factual or
fictional, whether they are spoken of in a comparitive way or not,
they always take place during sleep. This is also true of charismatic
-prophetic dreams ((Num. 12. 6-8: Joel 3.1). (16) Sleep or
slumber are presupposed. There is no case of a waking dream.
Developments of language which refer to dreaming taking place
when awake do no occur in biblical Hebrew. Interpretations
presupposing such development, are, as we expected,
anachronistic and therefore false. (17).

2.3 We can state positively that when the community in our
psalm expressly compares itself to 'dreamers' this can only mean
people who dream during sleep or slumber, who have dream
experiences which do not take place during their normal waking
state. Given the Old Testament evidence, the attempt to
understand Psalm 126, v. 1b must acknowledge this fact.

---

[15] For reconstructions of the text, cf. BHS. Following O. Kaum, *ATD* 18, 210.

[16] This includes dreams against which Jeremiah among others preaches. Cf.
Ehrlich BZAW, 155ff.

[17] Oppenheim's survey of the situation in the ancient Near East also supports this
fact. For the connection between the Akkadian *suttu* (dream) and *sittu* (sleep)
cf. op.cit., 225. See also op.cit., 187 and W. von Soden, AHw III, 1292.
1252.

2.4 Now we must enquire whether the comparison with dreamers refers to the self-deception of those who dream during sleep, the unreality of what is dreamt in sleep. As we saw, there is evidence in the Old Testament of the use of this negative valuation of the dream during sleep. Let us recall Psalm 73.20: the dream is transitory and what was dreamed is despised on waking. Let us recall Isaiah 29.7,8: The hungry and the thirsty who satisfy their desires only while dreaming, become painfully aware of their self-deception when they wake. (18)

Does Psalm 126, V.1b mean such self-deception? If we take the comparison 'we are like those who dream' literally, as it stands, then Zion — if we take this negative valuation of the dream — has deceived itself: 'We are like those who fell victim to a deception'. There is no question at all that the psalm writer could have meant this. No exegete has ever interpreted the passage in this way. Whenever a scholar accepted a negative of a dream in sleep, he has also assumed that Zion *feared*, feared without cause, that it had fallen victim to self-deception, such as happens in a dream. Thus — we must repeat — anyone who interprets the passage in this way, not only introduces thoughts that are nowhere in the text, but also refers, by introducing this fear, to a process in the waking state, a kind of waking dream (19) which is anachronistic from a linguistic-historical point of view. Therefore the simple equating of dreaming with self-deception misses the intention of the poem. The more complicated interpretation which offers a negative valuation and then negates it, cannot be considered because it is anachronistic. This means that all interpretations which use the negative valuation of the sleeping dream distort our meaning of the text. For the interpretation of our text, we are therefore left perforce with the *positive* valuation of the sleeping dream, which is strongly predominant in the Old Testament.

---

[18] Perhaps we should also mention Ec. 5.6 here. Cf. Ehrlich, BZAW, 164.

[19] See German Dictionary, 1450f (II a 1a).

2.5 By far the majority of the relevant texts are firmly convinced of the *reality* of what is dreamt. (20) There are several examples of this. What Abimelech sees in his sleeping dream cannot be doubted. It is faithfully carried out (Gen. 20. 3ff). What Joseph sees in his symbolic dream (21) and tells his brothers turns into reality (Gen. 37ff). What is dreamt in the Midianite camp, which Gideon overhears, soon proves to be true (Jud. 7.13, 14). What Solomon sees in a dream determines his reign (1 Kings 3. 5ff). In brief: the sleeping dream reveals what is or is coming or is to be. (22)

Neither is it usually disputed that *God* makes such a revelation possible through the medium of a dream, and thus also reveals himself. 'In a dream, in a vision of the night, ... while they slumber on their beds then he (God) opens the ears of men ...' (Job 33.15,16). (23) The God of Israel also reveals himself in dreams and visions to the prophets (Num. 12.6.) Of course this conviction is challenged by some, especially Jeremiah. (24) However this challenge is rare and certainly is not made by all the prophets. (25) As a rule the prophet of salvation is unshakeably certain that Jahweh speaks in dreams. Joel 3.1. is a striking example of this. (26)

Not in all but in many of the relevant texts the God-given

---

[20] J. Pedersen already stressed this point half a century ago: *Israel* I. II, 134f.

[21] For this type of dream cf. Ehrlich BZAW, pp. 58-124; also Oppenheim, op.cit., 206-212.

[22] For the latter, 'dream commands', cf. Ehrlich, op.cit., 125-136.

[23] German 'then he (God) reveals himself to men'. For the textual rendering cf. G. Fohrer, op.cit., 453f.

[24] Cf. 23.25-32: 27. 9-10: 29. 8-9. Cf. also on this point Ehrlich, op.cit., 155-70.

[25] In this context cf. A.R. Johnson, *The Cultic Prophet,* esp. 47ff.

[26] See also chap. 5.8.

dream reveals what is to come in the *future* or *shortly*. (27) Some examples of this are: Joseph's dreams (Gen. 37) prophesy the glittering future of the youngest of Jacob's sons, and symbolise his future dominance over his father and brothers. (28) Pharaoh's dream foretells the future of Egypt, seven good years followed by seven lean years (Gen. 41. 1-7); God foretells in dreams what he is about to do (Gen. 41.28). The man's dream in the Midianite camp is a sign of Israel's victory over it and foreshows an event decided upon by Jahweh but as yet still in the future, but which gives courage in the present (Judges 7.9ff, 13ff). The Babylonian King Nebuchadnezzar's dream also foretells what is to happen in the future (Dan. 2.29). Finally the charismatic dreams that Joel promises to all the people of Jahweh foretell the immediate future, and significantly, as well as dreaming, all will prophesy (Joel 3.1).(29) Both God-given dreams and prophecy are signs that will happen before 'the day of Jahweh' comes (Joel 3.1-4). This shows how often in the Old Testament a dream is sent by God to foreshow the future, what God intends to do. In Judges 7 and Joel 3 we see how the saving change can be experienced in advance in a dream. (30)

---

27 Cf. F. Schmidtke, *Traüme*, 240-246. For the ancient Near East, see especially A.L. Oppenheim, op.cit., esp. chapter 7: 'Mantic Dreams', 237ff and 185.

28 Cf. Ehrlich, BZAW, 64.

29 Cf. W. Rudolph, KAT XIII 2, 72.

30 We should not ignore the fact that this is also true for all the ancient East. For the sake of brevity we refer the reader to Oppenheim, op.cit. Particularly noteworthy is El's dream in which he foresees a turn of events in a dream, so realistically and convincingly that he at once rejoices and opens his mouth (?) to laugh (CTA 6, III-VI = IAB, III-IV = Gordon 49, III-VI; K.-H. Bernhardt, *Ugaritische Texte,* 236f. Note also that he, a god, is dreaming, cf. Oppenheim, op.cit., 212f). It is worth comparing with a Mesopotamian poem *Ludlul bêl nêmeqi,* in which a suffering righteous man near death has a

2.6 Once we know how the ancient Israelites spoke about dreams and dreaming, what they meant by it, the true meaning of our psalm verse follows, as if of its own accord! The people in the psalm poem compare themselves to those who experience beforehand, in a God-given dream, what Jahweh intends to do. (31) The restoration of Zion (32) is in the future. More precisely, it is a fact already decided on by God, and thus in this sense already real, but for normal human experience still latent, hidden in the future. The community of Zion expressly compares itself to dreamers who perceive through God's will the still hidden reality: 'we are like dreamers' meaning: like dreamers we see Jahweh restoring Zion, we already know that then our mouth will be filled with laughter and our tongue with shouts of joy, we already hear it said among the nations: 'The Lord has done great things for them!' and because of what we foresee in this dream, we too can say: 'The Lord has done great things for us'. The God-given experience in advance makes us rejoice now in the present: 'we *are* like dreamers' (verse 1b) and therefore: 'we *are* glad.' (verse 3b). Because of this advance experience, our present state looks quite different to us.

Thus verses 1-3 of the psalm refer *both* to the present and the future. The dream-like anticipating is in the present, the joy deriving from it is present, and the change of circumstances which God has already decided upon, still hidden in him but

---

series of dreams in which he foresees a change for the better (Tab III. In W.G. Lambert, *Babylonian Wisdom Literature* 47ff. See also 23f and Oppenheim, op.cit., 250 and 217.). We should also note that penitential psalms of the same region not only pray for the banishment of pain but also for the grace-giving dream which would foreshow inevitable to come (Text according to *St Langdon, Babylonian Wisdom* (129-229),143; cf. also H. Zimmern, *Babylonische Busspsalmen,* 101.105. I would also like to thank my Munster colleague W. von Soden for kind information about this).

[31] W.O.E. Osterley's interpretation (among others) thus comes nearest to the meaning of the text: op.cit., p. 515.

[32] See below chap 4.1.

charismatically foreshadowed, is also present. But its manifestation in the ordinary world, and normal experience of it, is still in the future. Thus 'being like dreamers' makes perfect sense in the context. (33) Moreover it is the key to understanding the psalm, the interpenetation of the present and the future, the interplay of perfect and imperfect, the constellation of all verb forms. (34) To those who foresee like dreamers, everything is already a *fait accompli*. To those experiencing normal everyday life, it is still in the future. The phrase 'we are like dreamers' is thus the hinge linking the two parts of the psalm: because what is foreseen in a dream is not yet normally manifest, being still to come, there follows the *prayer*: 'Restore our fortunes.' (verse 4), (35) and further requires the *promise* (verse 5f.): 'He that goes forth weeping, bearing the seed for sowing, shall come home with shouts of joy ...' Understood in this way, the tension between the two halves of the psalm which gave the exegetes so much trouble, no longer irritates. Now it is merely the tension between what is dreamt and normal experience, or more precisely, between dream-like anticipation and normal everyday experience. Understanding of verse 1b is basically quite simple and is supported by its context. We have only to regret that the unfortunate Honi, the drawer of circles, spent his whole life worrying about it!

---

[33] Contrary to the opinion of M. Dahood, op.cit., pp. 218-9.

[34] Cf. chap 3.3.

[35] It is worth comparing this to the first two visions of Amos (7.1-3, 4-6). In them misfortune, which the Lord has already ordained, is foreseen (cf. Amos 7.2a BHS). However, the prophet prays (successfully) that it should not become manifest in normal life. Correspondingly our psalm anticipates salvation. And the community prays that it should become fully manifest in normal experience. Salvation or misfortune, which are as yet hidden in God, although already real, still leave room for human prayer and pleading; they do not demand deterministic acceptance but prayerful involvement for or against them.

3. The Linguistic Form

Here we confine ourselves to the most necessary task: we confirm our previous findings on the grammatical and syntactic level, (1) we discuss the question of literary form (2) and we analyse the structure of our poem in order to have a satisfactory starting point.

3.1. For our structural analysis we begin with the rhythm. The first four lines of the psalm (3) are hexameters (senars) (4) the last four verses are mainly pentameters (Qina). If we follow the meaning breaks within the verses for pauses in the rhythm, (5) we only get clear caesurae in the first four verses, and in verse 5 in the second half. The pentameters, of which there are three (v. 4, 6a and 6b), are all 'single phrase pentameters' and there is no noticeable meaning or rhythm break in them. (6) Thus the poem

---

[1] See above chap. 1.2.

[2] See above chap. 1.3.

[3] Here as elsewhere, the editorial title is not considered.

[4] If we follow J. Morgenstern's principle, op.cit., 111, this also goes for the third line.

[5] Cf. L. Alonso-Schökel, *Das Alte Testament als literarisches Kunstwerk,* 140-1.

[6] In Begrich's analysis these three are all examples of the type 1 pentameter: Cf. J. Begrich, ZS 9, 171ff. See also ThB 21, 134ff.

[7] Fundamentally the senar is divided according to the formula 3 + 3, but when the content requires, it can follow the formula 4 + 2 or 2 + 4, without losing the feeling of unity in the hexameter. See L. Alonso-Schökel, op.cit., 41. (see over page)

[8] We wish to follow the Masoretic text in verse 6a, but find only two stresses in it. However we agree with the Masoretes who 'unstressed' the middle word through Maqqef, see over page.

C

falls into two clearly different parts, which we can summarise as follows (see footnotes 7 and 8, p. 25)

Part I	verse 1:	$4 + 2 = 6$	
	verse 2a:	$4 + 2 = 6$	
	verse 2b:	$2 + 4 = 6$	
	verse 3:	$4 + 2 = 6$	(7)
Part II	verse 4:	$(3 + 2 =) 5$	
	verse 5:	$2 + 2 = 4$	
	verse 6a:	$(3 + 2 =) 5$	(8)
	verse 6b:	$(3 + 2 =) 5$	

3.2. Part I is also separated from Part II by the stylistic device of 'enclosure'. The clauses *hajînu k^{e}hol^{e}mîm* (v. 1b) and *hajînu s^{e}mehim* (v. 3b) are similarly structured and they rhyme, they correspond to one another and by their position in the first and last lines 'enclose' Part I of the poem. In their relationship to one another they also build up to a climax. First the people of Zion are 'like dreamers', then they are 'filled with gladness'. There is no doubt that Part I of our psalm has a more regular than Part II. It is concentrated and tightly woven, not only, but chiefly by anaphora. (10) The particle 'az joined to an imperfect is repeated at the beginning of the successive verses 2a and 2b. The phrase *higdîl jhwh la sôt ^{c}im* is repeated in vv. 2b and 3. If we compare this with Part II of the poem, we see that Part I with its visible delight in the stylistic device of the anaphora has a stylistic individuality which distinguishes it from Part II. Thus the two part nature of our psalm is made plain by stylistic devices, but it is also a stylistic device which links the two parts together: the device of beginning each part with the same theme introduced by the same word. (11)

---

[9] Cf. W. Bühlmann - K. Scherer, *Stilfiguren der Bibel,* 30.

[10] Cf. Bühlmann - K. Scherer, op.cit., 27.

[11] Cf. again, Bühlmann-Scherer, op.cit., 23.

The term *sûb s^eb̂ût*, which is so important to the psalm, introduces both Part I and Part II and thus links them together (Vv. 1 and 4): Zion's restoration (12) is experienced by anticipation (Part I) and prayed for in its manifestation (Part II). Parallel to this the word 'joy' *(rinnā)* is also an important theme word to the psalm. It is repeated three times (v. 2a, 5, 6) and thus recurs through both halves of the text. In Part I, Zion's joy is foreseen, in Part II it is hoped for in tears. Thus from the stylistic devices we deduce that our Psalm is divided into two Parts (verses 1-3 and 4-6) but that it is also an organic unity.

3.3. Once we have made clear the structure of the poem, then the interpretation we gave in 2.6. can also be confirmed grammatically and syntactically. The two sides of the 'enclosure' we mentioned (v. 1b and 3b) describe *present* conditions. The people who are speaking in this psalm are present, here and now while the psalm is being recited, they are like dreamers who anticipate the future. Because of this they are 'joyful', now while the psalm is sounding. The twice used perfect *hajînû* is stative and functions in its own particular way. (13) It *can* refer to the present. Gen. 42.9, 11, 31 is a common but particularly convincing example. The question between Joseph and his brothers is not what the latter *were* in the past but what they *are* in the present. 'We are honest men, we are not spies (as Joseph had suggested).' *lo'hajînû m^eragg ^elîm.* (v. 31) This should leave no further doubt that *hajînû* can refer to the present. (14) There is no grammatical or syntactic problem of the interpretation given here to the comparison with dreamers. According to this interpretation of the text, verses 1a, 2 and 3a are — in one sense! — still *future:* 'When the Lord restores Zion ... our mouth is full of laughter ... our

---

[12] For this interpretation of the expression, see below, chap. 4.1.

[13] Cf. R. Meyer, *Hebräische Grammatik,* 1,20; III, 49ff.

[14] Many may think this is flogging a dead horse. But, as the debates mentioned have shown, it is still necessary to give it.

tongue with shouts of joy; then they say among the *gôjim* ...'
Here we too can prove the grammatical and syntactic possibility of
this: The twice used 'az with imperfect *can*, when it follows a
previous sentence which begins with *be* plus an infinitive
construct refer to future time. Proverbs 1.27f. is excellent proof of
this! When the sentence referring to the present *hajînû kehol emîm*
(we are like dreamers) stands between two sentences referring to
the future, it is *parenthetical.* Not everything at the beginning of
the psalm refers to the future: the introductory phrase about the
restoration of Zion does (v.1a), the praise and recognition in the
following part does (v. 2a and 2b) but not the remark (now!) that
we are like dreamers (v. 1b). This latter interrupts the future
context and therfore is logically parenthetical. There is no denying
that biblical Hebrew does make use of such parentheses. (15) A
well known and outstanding example of these kind of parentheses
is the syntactic structure of the beginning of the Jahvist account of
creation (Gen. 4b-7). (16) However we can not only prove that
v.1b as a parentheses is linguistically possible in Hebrew, there are
various signs — on grounds of linguistic form — that it must be
taken so. Firstly the comparison with Prov. 1.27f. and Job 33.15f.
shows that first parts of a sentence with the construction *be* plus
the infinitive construct very often are allowed by a second part of
the sentence beginning with 'az plus the imperfect: 'when panic
strikes you ...' *(be....),* 'when distress and anguish come upon you'
(17) *(bebo ...),* 'then they will call upon me'... *('az jiqra'ûnnî ...)'* or
'when deep sleep falls upon men ... *(binpol...)* 'then he (God) opens
the ears of men ... *('az jiglae...).* Comparison with these texts
show, I think, that in our psalm too the first part of the sentence
besûb 'ät-sîbat sijjôn (when the Lord restores the fortunes of Zion) is
not completed till the *'az jimmale'* (then our mouth is filled)... and
'az jo'merû (then they say) ... rather than in the phrase *hajînû*

---

[15] Not only those mentioned by C. Brockelmann, *Hebräische Syntax* 164, para.
175, which are verbs of speaking in the context of direct speech.

[16] Verses 5-6 interrupt the sentence in verses 4b and 7.

[17] Thus Zöckler following B. Gemser, HAT I, 16.22. Translator has used RSV.

keḥol ᵉmîm (we are like dreamers). The latter is parenthetical. Secondly we must remember the tendency to use the stylistic device of anaphora in Part I. (18) If the state of being like dreamers (v. 1b) was a *consequence* of the restoration of Zion (v. 1a) just as joy and rejoicing (v. 2a) and recognition among the *gojîm* (v. 2b) are, then following the pattern of anaphora, all three consequences would have to be introduced by 'az plus the imperfect and not just the (so-called) second and third. If the anaphoristic form is only used in verses 2a and 2b, and verse 1b is perfect (which interrupts the syntax), then I think this is also an indication that the half verse 1b is distinct from the consequences (of the restoration of Zion) in verses 2a and 2b and thus a parenthesis. Thirdly, but not least, we should note that verses 1b and 3b are corresponding sides of the 'enclosure' we mentioned (19) and therefore stand out from the train of thought in Part 1. This also suggests a certain hiatus before and after verses 1b and 3b and thus the parenthetical character of the former. In short we can say that our interpretation of the psalm in which being like dreamers is a present state and Zion's restoration with its accompanying joy and recognition is an anticipated future, can be completely supported on the grammatical and syntactic level: verse 1b is not only philologically possible as a parenthesis but there are many signs that the possible is both actual and appropriate here.

Thus we have proved linguistically what previous debate (20) demanded explicit verification of. (Part II of the poem does not require further commentary from the grammatical and syntactic point of view).

3.4. The question of literary form is also clarified (21). For: our interpretation of the psalm does not permit us to hold that it has liturgical structures. The certainty that the Lord will restore Zion

---

[18] See above chap. 3.2.

[19] See above chap. 3.2.

[20] See above chap. 1.2.

[21] See above chap. 1.3.

is not offered through a cultic service, or proclaimed by a prophetic or priestly speaker, but grasped by the community itself — in a God-given anticipation of bold faith, a pre-experience through becoming like dreamers. The communal 'we' used in both the first and the second half of the psalm (22) corresponds to this. The grammar completely supports this disputed solution.

Neither are the closing verses 5 and 6 liturgical. They articulate what those who belong to Zion grasp by anticipating. They who have experienced in advance God's restoring action, and the recognising, rejoicing reaction of men to it, know — through this anticipatory experience — that the tears that are still wept now are 'seeds' from which the 'harvest' will grow. Psalm 126 is not a liturgical poem. Neither does it mimic liturgy.

Nor is it a people's lament. What the community experiences in advance is not cause for lamentation. The first half of the text is about recognition, laughing and rejoicing (in advance!). According to half verse 3b the present is a condition of gladness. The second half of the psalm says that tears still flow. But in the light of the salvation to come they are seen as seed for the harvest and thus overcome by faith and no longer a reason for lament. The way in which Part II is rhythmically divided (23) seems, at least to some extent, to reflect this. If the Qînâ rhythm in Part II of the psalm suggests sadness (24) we should note that it is interrupted: the proclamation of the certainty of faith that those who sow in tears will reap in joy is expressed significantly in a different rhythm. (25) Although neither Part I nor Part II can be described as a people's lament, there is no doubt (and no philological difficulty) (26) that the psalm includes a prayer of petition (v.4): The community prays that God *will* do what he intends. (27) The

---

²² See verses 1b, 2a, 3 and (in Part II) v.4.

²³ See above chap. 3.1.

²⁴ I only suggest this, but am not sure myself.

²⁵ 2 + 2

²⁶ See M. Dahood, op.cit., 218, 220.

second half of the text gives place, not to a people's lament but to a prayer of petition. (28) The anticipation of salvation includes, rather than excludes, the community being moved to pray that what they have anticipated should be made manifest as soon as possible. The element of prayer of petition in this case must go together with the declaration of trust (v.5 and v.6.)

Thus all in all, the form critical analysis is clear. The fact that it is hard to put one of the available names of literary forms to our findings is another matter. Perhaps we could say that Part I can be described as a kind of making present of salvation, in which hymnic elements play a not unimportant part,(29) Part II is an accompanying prayer of petition linked with expressions of trust.

This makes it very difficult to draw conclusions about the psalm's place in life.(30) Of course the communal 'we' style suggests that the poem was recited in the communal cult (as has already been said). But it is not possible to be more precise than this. However there is no doubt that the psalmist speaks of seed and harvest in a purely metaphorical sense and that here a prayer for rain (31) plays no part, or at least no part worth mentioning.(32) This means that the suggestion of a special cult festival of Jahweh has no support in the text.

Although this is as far as we can go here, we can still attempt to put the psalm in its historical context. In which historical moment did it arise and survive?

---

[27] See above chapter 2, note 35.

[28] This example makes clear - once again! - the difference between a (people's) lament and a prayer of petition. What sense does it make to insist that when-ever there is a petition in the psalm, it is a lament? Isn't it impossible to have a prayer of petition which does not bear the character of a lament? In the present case I think this is important. Cf. on this, the author in FRLANT 99, 154f.

[29] Cf. vv. 2-3.

[30] Cf. above chap 1.4.

[31] Cf. A.A. Anderson, op.cit., 864.

[32] More on this in chap. 5.9.

4. The Historical Context

4.1 The words that once appeared to offer a clue to the historical context have proved to be a philological mistake. The expression *sîbat sijjôn* in the first half verse of the psalm has nothing — almost certainly — to do with *sbh* ('taken away into captivity') and thus does not mean the people of Zion in captivity, as once the Septuagint and Vulgate supposed and as many commentators still hold. (1) An ancient Aramaic text of a state treaty, discovered in *Sefîre* a place in Syria, contains this disputed word in exactly the same consonantal grouping 2 *(sjbt)* (2) and in the context in which it is used together with the Haphel of the clearly root-related *swb,*leaves no doubt at all that it refers to the restoration of an original state, *restitutio in integrum.* (3) What was already probable from the textual data available in the Old Testament where the expression is used (4) can now be taken as certain. The term *sûbs^e^bût* (and its variants) (5) does not mean the bringing back of deported captives; neither *sûb 'ät-sîbat sijôn* in Psalm 126.1. nor the corresponding prayer in 126.4. refer to the homecoming from the Babylonian exile. (It is quite another question, which in the

---

1 Cf. Buttenwieser, op.cit., 283, 287. See also, apparently, M. Mannasti, op.cit., 150.

2 According to S. Segret the word may once have been pronounced Sajjábat: *Archiv Orientalni* 32 (127-131) 126. For the sefire (Stele III, line 24) cf.●A. Dupont-Sommer (and J. Starky), *Une inscription araméenne,* esp. 27, 30, 35. See also J.A. Fitzmyer, *The Aramaic Inscriptions of Sefîre,* 100-101, 119-120.

3 The context, which is about the restoration (within normal historical time!) of a decimated land owner class can be found in German translation in E. Lipunski, *Religionsgeschichtlichen Textbuch zum Alten Testament,* 282. Details of the text, op.cit. 272f.

4 See E.L. Dietrich, BZAW 40, esp. 12-28. However E. Baumann's slightly later argument ZAW 47, 17-44, came to a different conclusion, (the annulment of a decree of imprisonment for debt).

5 Its textual rendering is very complicated. Cf. R. Borger, ZAW 66, 315-6.

circumstances is worth considering, whether a returning from exile may have been part of the intended *restitutio in integrum* among other things! Whatever the answer to this question, it is still quite clear that in our psalm neither verse 1 nor verse 4 refer specifically to the homecoming from exile.) This disposes of the hypotheses based on the verb *sbh,* which date the psalm shortly before or after the return from exile in Babylon, that is to say in the last third of the sixth century B.C. Once again we see that dating the psalms is not quite a simple matter. The historical context of a poem, in our present case too, can only be determined indirectly: through the limits required by the history of traditions and themes. So for this indirect approach, let us investigate the relationship between elements of our psalm text and other Old Testament writings.

4.2. Of course not every theme or linguistic expression can help us to date our psalm. Although 126.2 speaks of a 'mouth filled with laughter' and 'tongues with shouts of joy' exactly like the poem in Job (Job 8.21), this does not tell us very much. The final words of the psalm about coming home with shouts of joy is similar to Is. 51.11 but we cannot conclude anything from this. Such similarities in theme and expression are too casual and fleeting to allow us to draw any conclusions about the psalm's date.

4.3. If we take the expression *sûb 'ät sîbat* or *sûb s^ebût* (126.1,4) this does not help much either. Of course it is a striking expression. But it is too common and in use for too long to be able to tell us anything precise about the date of our psalm. We should recall that this expression, in its ancient Aramaic form, was already in use in inscriptions in the Old Testament world by the eighth century B.C. (6) We see from two passages in the Book of Twelve Prophets (Amos. 9.14 and Hos. 6.11) that it was already in use within the Old Testament during that same century. (7) Jeremiah

---

[6] Sefîre Stele III, line 24.

[7] See W. Rudolph's convincing argument for the conclusion of Amos, KAT XIII 2, pp. 278-287, esp. p. 285f. See also H.W. Wolff, BK XIV/1, pp. 132,

30. 3, 18 is an example of the expression's use at the end of the 7th century. (8) Joel 4.1. shows its use at the beginning of the 6th century B.C. (9) Examples for the period after 587, the year of catastrophe for the Southern Kingdom, are unquestionably frequent. Although it is difficult to distinguish between expressions used during the exile and those which are post-exilic (10) here there is no question that the expression we are considering was used frequently in *both* periods. For the period of the exile we have Dtn. 30.3; Ez. 16. 53 and Lam. 2.14 (11) and probably also secondary Jeremiah texts such as 31.23 or 33.11. For the use of the expression in the post-exilic period, Jer. 29.14, 33.7; Zeph. 2.7c; Ps. 14.7 (53.7) and Job 42.2 are fairly certain examples. (12) In short, it is clear that the term *sûb 'ät-sîbat,* respectively *sûb sebut,* was used over many centuries and therefore

---

138, 157. Rudolph's opinion of the Hosean text starts with the assumption that the restoration meant in this expression was *always* a 'unique, sudden and saving change', that is to say unrepeatable (KAT XIII 1, 143f.) Should this assumption which is undoubtedly correct for the mass of later Old Testament examples, also hold good for a much earlier period? The Sefire example (8th century B.C.) does not make it clear that, at this early period, this is the only tenable interpretation of the expression. The Sefire text refers to a restoration which takes place within the normal course of history and is of course repeatable.

[8] See W. Rudolph, HAT I 12, 172.

[9] Cf. A.S. Kapelrud, *Joel Studies,* esp. 191 and also W. Rudolph, KAT XIII 2 esp. 26. See also under chap. 5.5.

[10] Especially I think with reference to Jer. 32.44; 33.26; 48.47; 49.6, 39; Es. 29.14 and Zeph. 3.20.

[11] Apart from the fact that the verb here is in hiphil, the expression as a whole is used, uncommonly, to refer to a different subject (not Jahweh, but Zion's prophets).

[12] Ps. 85.2 is omitted purposely. A full but no longer up to date account of this is to be found in E.L. Dietrich, op.cit. 12-28.

is not of great help in our attempt to date our psalm. At any rate, if we consider the fact that exilic and post-exilic examples of this term are by far the most frequent, this suggests that this late period is the most probable date for the composition of our psalm. We have no surer indication than this.

4.4. Research continues to investigate in which historical period the name Zion became common in the way it is used in Ps. 126.1. (13) In order to establish what it means in verse 1, we begin with the fact that it is identical in form and meaning in verse 1a and 4a. (14) It goes without saying that the *restitutio in integrum* refers to the same object in both verses. The community of God speaking in verse 4a say 'Restore us Lord!' and thus prays for *its* own restoration; it follows that the half verse 1a must also refer to the restoration of the community of God: this is what 'Zion' means. Whether or no it also refers to the temple of the Lord on the mountain of the same name, as the life centre of this sacral community, this does not alter the fact that 'Zion' in 126.1... refers primarily to this community in South Palestine. We should also note that it is not referred to in a threatening way, but in a reverent way, in the hope of its restoration. In short 'Zion' means the community of faith hoping for its restoration, the community which is centred on Zion and therefore calls itself 'Zion'. If we return to our opening question, when did the name 'Zion' become commonly used in this sense, our answer is that this happened, as far as we can see during the time of Deutero-Isaiah. (15) For reasons that would take too long to give here, (16) the newly awakening hope after the destruction of the Southern Kingdom was centred on Jerusalem and Zion. At the same time, with the personalisations of 'daughter of Jersualem' and 'daughter

---

[13] For the many usages of this name see F. Stolz, *Zion*.

[14] See above no. 3.2.

[15] Cf. Cf. N.W. Porteous, *Jerusalem-Zion* (1961) 246ff., (1967) 105ff.

[16] Cf. instead, N.W. Porteous, op.cit., 236-244 or 94-103.

of Zion' (17) 'Jerusalem' and 'Zion' embodied the community of the Lord. Leaving aside the use of the name of Jersualem in our context, we find that 'Zion' as a name for the community hoping for restoration appears in the proclamation of the prophet Deutro-Isaiah. Is. 49.14ff. and 52.1ff. show a use of the word Zion identical with that in our psalm. (Is. 48.1,2 reproaches expressly those who belong to Jacob/Israel/Judah and 'call themselves after the holy city'). (18) Thus it is clear that in the days of Deutro-Isaiah, that is to say during the Babylonian exile, the name Zion precisely as it is used in our psalm became common usage. However this only gives us a *terminus a quo* because 'Zion' is used very similarly in Trito-Isaiah.

4.5. A helpful phrase for dating our psalm comes in Ps. 126.2: 'Then they said among the nations; (19) The Lord has done great things for them!' It is plain what this means. The psalm repeats and transforms what the *gôjim* said *before* circumstances changed, before the restoration of Zion. When the Lord restores Zion, then the scorn the *gôjim* poured on Zion abandoned by her God, will be silenced. This gives us the background to our psalm. To put it plainly, the theme is not just the despising of the Lord's community. If it were no more than this, the thought would be too widespread in the Old Testament to give us anything definite

---

[17] Cf. Lam. 1.6; 2.1,4,8,10 (11), 13,15,18 and e.g. also Is. 1.8, Mic. 1.13. See H. Wh. Robinson, *The Hebrew Conception of the corporate personality*. It is also noteworthy in this context that Joel 2.23, on the threshold of the exilic period (cf. below chap. 5.5.) apostrophises the 'Son of Zion'. W. Rudolph's conjecture about Joel 1.8 is too uncertain to bear any weight in this research; KAT III 2, 37,39.)

[18] This brings out the identity between 'Jerusalem' and 'Zion'.

[19] To omit *baggôjim* (among the nations) *metri causa:* cannot be justified either by textual or literary criticism. Up to a certain point with J. Morgenstern, op.cit., 111f. Cf. above chap. 3.1. especially Part 3, note 4. Against this W.O.E. Oesterley, op.cit., 515 and e.g. B. Duhm, op.cit., 436f. (The latter calls the phrase a 'correctly explanatory gloss'.)

enough to pin an historical context on. (20) More precisely, the *gôjim,* the heathen, the nations, the neighbouring peoples (in general) still despise and mock and scorn the unfortunate community abandoned by its God.

If we try to take our bearings from this theme, we must inquire when was the community in this state? It appears first, we think, in the final years before 587. The prophetic warnings in Jer. 24.9 and Ez. 5.8 refer to this period, and possibly also Ez. 22.4, 16. (21) The lament in Joel 2.17 and the corresponding comforting in Joel 2.19 also refer to this time. (22) *After* 587 during the period of the Babylonian exile, the theme plays an even greater part. Especially in communal lamentation. We may quote passages from the exilic Psalms 44.14, 15: (23) 'Thou hast made us a byword among the nations, a laughing stock among the peoples ...' Ps. 79.4 (24) to see clearly the meaning of what the nations said and their mockery during this period of exile. We merely add some analogous examples of how the nations mocked the Lord's community taken from the historical writings, also during the exilic period (Dtn. 28.36, 37; 29.23; 1 Kings 9.7.) This theme was especially common during the exile and also during the decade before it. (26) However, it is still too early to draw conclusions

---

[20] The theme goes back to very early times: cf. e.g. 1 Sam. 11.2; 17.26. A very late example on the other hand is Neh. 2.17.

[21] For this dating cf. W. Rudolph, HAT I 12, 145 on the one hand and W. Zimmerli, BK XIII/1, 135ff and 506f.

[22] The author agrees with the dating of W. Rudolph (KAT XIII 2, 24-9). Cf. below chap. 5.5.

[23] For the contextualisation of the psalm 44.10-27. cf. W. Beyerlin, *Innerbiblische Aktualisierungsversuche,* 456f.

[24] Cf. by the way R.C. Culley, *Oral Formulatic Language* 76 (System IIIa.b.)

[25] We could also quote Pss. 74.19, 18, 22; 79.12.

[26] The events of the years 597 were cause enough in themselves. The question 'why' in Ps. 79.10 is repeated after the exile in Ps. 115.2. but clearly with another meaning. This passage does not justify us in extending the period

from this about the historical situation of Psalm 126. We note that this poem repeats this theme by reversing it. The theme of what the nations say remains. But *what* they say has become positive: The nations no longer express scorn, but recognition, and even praise, praise for the God who has restored Zion. Is there anything similar of about this date anywhere else in the Old Testament? In fact there is, again in texts from the exilic period! Ezechiel, the prophet of this period, has this theme and its reversal into the positive. In 36.15. the Lord says: 'I will not let you hear any more the reproach of the nations, and you shall no longer bear the disgrace of the people's ...' (27) The school of Ezechiel kept this promise alive up until the late stages of the exilic period (Ez. 34.29). (28) And this promise goes together with this prophet's stereotyped proclamations of a God jealous for salvation who does not want his reputation, his 'name' to be ill-spoken of by the nations *(leᶜênê haggôjim)* (Ez. 20.9, 14, 22, 41 etc). (29) The other prophet of exile, Deutero-Isaiah, makes the Lord act to save his people, expressly 'before the eyes of all nations' (Is. 52.10). (30) This yearning of the Lord's community at that time also comes out in the exilic reinterpretation of the Psalm 102. (31) Here the community longs that the nations no longer despise the Lord's name, that they reverence it again and recognise his glory (Ps. 120.16). Thus it was a notable aspect of the exilic period (32) that the community minded very much what the nations said about the

---

during which this theme was used to the time after the exile.

[27] On this oracle of salvation see W. Zimmerli, BK XIII/2, 851, 860. Cf. also the context in 36.6,7.

[28] See W. Zimmerli, op.cit., 847.

[29] For its particular use in the exile situation see W. Zimmerli, op.cit., 441 and 453. The phrase *leᶜênê haggôjim* also occurs in the contemporary compilation P2 of the law of holiness Lev. 26.45. See K. Elliger HAT I 4, 379.

[30] According to this prophet, he gives his glory to no other: Is. 42.8; 48.11.

[31] On this see J. Becker, *Israel deutet seine Psalmen,* 43-5.

[32] Including a few years before it, with regard to Ez. 20.9, 14, 22 and Joel 2.19b.

Lord. It was a theme of *this* period that they mocked, but also that through the Lord's zealous action 'before the eyes of the nations' their mockery stopped. This massively supported fact is opposed by a single text that must be post-exilic in the version that has come down to us. This is Ps. 98. In verses 2 and 3 it takes up — probably because of a reworking inspired by Is. 52.10 — the theme of the exilic period again. As it is the only one, it can hardly disturb our impression that this theme is characteristic of the exilic period. In the light of this finding it is very possible that our text Psalm 126.2 together with the whole psalm was composed during the exilic period. The provenance of the phrase *sûb s^ebût* suggested a late origin of our psalm, the way in which the name Zion was used gave us the exilic period as a *terminus a quo,* and now this reference to what the nations said, completely convinces us that Psalm 126 was composed during the exilic period and neither earlier nor later. Other points in the psalm confirm this. The prayer for restoration (v.4.) and especially the picture of a long time sowing in tears, (v.5 and 6a) allow us, without any doubt at all, to deduce the exilic situation. We are not compelled to but almost. Nothing in the poem goes against the exilic dating, which its themes, as we have said, recommend.

5. Its Context in the History of Tradition

5.1 The finding of when, in which historical period, the themes characterising our psalm were used have enabled us to define the historical context in which this psalm with its various themes can most probably be situated. It also gives us another insight: that of the history of tradition. It brought out in which traditions the themes of our psalm were used. If we look back we find one constant impression throughout: the themes in question occur usually, if not always in prophetic contexts. This goes for the term *sûb 'ät - sîbat* (and *sûb s^ebut*). It is not, as the Sefire text shows, an exclusively prophetic term. Even within the Old Testament it is not the private property of the prophets. (1) But as far as we can tell, it was used first by the prophets, (2) and current for many centuries in their proclamation. (3) On the other hand the way in which Psalm 126 uses the name Zion is only found elsewhere among the prophets: especially in Deutro-Isaiah (4) and again in Trito-Isaiah. (5) Finally the exception that the Lord will put an end to the mockery of the nation is found, with one exception (6) exclusively among the prophets: Joel (7) and Ezechiel, the school of Ezechiel (8) and not least also in Deutro-Isaiah. (9) It is not

---

1 Cf. its non-prophetic use in Dtn. 30.3 - Ps. 14.7 (53.7); 85.2; Job 42.2 and varied in Lam. 2.14.

2 Am. 9.14; Hos. 6.11. Cf. again Part 4 note 7.

3 Jer. 29.14; 30.3, 18; 31.23; 32.44; 33.7, 11, 26; 48.47; 49.6, 39; Ez. 16.53; 29.14; Joel 4.1; Zeph. 2.7; 3.20.

4 Is. 49.14ff; 52.1ff and 48.1.f.

5 We should also recall the formulation in Joel 2.23. which comes near to the usage.

6 Ps. 102.16.

7 2.2. 19b.

8 Ez. 20.9, 14, 22, 41-34.29; 39.15.

9 Is. 42.8; 48.11; 52.10.

without significance that these elements in our psalm are — either exclusively or predominantly — used by the prophets. These leads to the suggestion that Psalm 126 itself comes from *prophetic* sources.

5.2. Now we enquire, to be more complete, *where,* in which *geographical* space was the reception of these themes possible? Where were they 'current'? We want to find out more about the provenance of our psalm. For all the themes we have investigated the answer is: they were current *both* in Babylonian exile and at home in Palestine. Firstly the term *sûb sᵉbut* was, as shown by its use in the books of Jeremiah, Zephaniah and Joel, (10) in use in Jerusalem and Judah. It was also used, as the Ezechiel texts show (11) in exilic circles. Secondly, the way in which our psalm speaks of Zion was, going by Joel and Lamentations, (12) already becoming current in Jerusalem at the beginning of the exile. (13) On the other hand, it is used in fully developed form by Deutero-Isaiah, (14) that is to say in the Gola in Babylonia. Thirdly the expectation that the Lord will put an end to the nations' mockery is found in both places: Joel 2.18, 19 and Ps. 102.16 are examples from Judah-Jerusalem. (15) Deutero-Isaiah and Ezechiel texts come from the Babylonian exile. (16) Thus it is clear that all the above themes were current both at home and in exile. A conclusion about the provenance of our psalm is not possible on this evidence.

---

[10] Cf. Jer. 29.14; 30.3, 18; 31.23; 33.7, 11; Zeph. 2.7; 3.20; Joel 4.1. See also Lam. 2.14.

[11] Cf. 16.53; 29.14.

[12] Cf. Joel 2.23 - Lam. 1.6; 2.1, 4, 8, 10 etc.

[13] It is important that later usage became identical.

[14] Cf. Is. 48.1f. - 49.14ff. - 52.1ff.

[15] For the provenance of the reinterpreted psalm cf. 102.15, 17, 22.

[16] Cf. Is. 42.8 - 48.11 and especially 52.10. See also Ez. 20.9, 14, 22, 41 etc; 34.29; 36.15.

5.3. Another theme we have not yet mentioned seems to be more helpful, the one in 126.4b. It compares the restoration of Zion to the water-courses in the Negeb, comparing the 'aphîkîm of South Judah, which when they run with water (17) are restored in their fashion. In this theme don't we have the geographical environment of our poet, his range of experience which colours his ideas and wishes? Even if we wanted to say yes to this, there is still the difficulty that the poet could also be a South Palestinian deported to the rivers of Babylon. (18) This means that this theme is not certain evidence that we can place the psalm in the Judah-Jerusalem environment.

5.4. Greater certainty about the psalm's regional and traditional provenance comes from other research: the detailed comparison with the proclamation of the prophet Joel. (19) This comparison is important because it does not rest on just one or two points but on a constellation of themes, a complex of thoughts. In Joel 2.17 we find concern about the nations' mockery, about 'what is said among the nations'. Joel 2.18 speaks of God's jealousy; he will not endure this mockery. Joel 2.19. says that the Lord's people will be released from being 'a reproach among the nations'. All in all, a straight correspondance with our psalm, a factual and sometimes word for word correspondence, as between 126.2 and Joel 2.21 when instead of mockery, it will be said: 'The Lord has done great things' *higdîl jhwh la* $^{c\acute{a}}$*sôt*. Is it not significant that this formulation only occurs in one other place in the Old Testament?

---

[17] Cf. e.g., B.Y. Aharoni, *The Land of the Bible*, 24.

[18] This possible also because the theme seems to have played a part in the tradition. Cf. below chap 5.4.

[19] Up till now this research has been hindered through wrong presuppositions. This goes for the views put forward in J. Morgenstern's special study, op.cit., 115-116, 110-111. Joel 2.20f is compared in different ways by F. Baethgen, op.cit. 381 and H. Gunkel, op.cit. 551.

(20) namely in Ps. 126.2b? This is clearly a second significant connection between our two texts. Moreover the phrase 'The Lord has done great things to them' (the members of the Zion community) is expressed in both places by ^casa $^cim:$ Joel 2.26; Ps. 126.2b, 3. Although in this case the choice of words is not so rare in the Old Testament, (21) taken together with the other points, it can be called a third connection between the two passages. Joel's use of 'Sons of Zion' (2.23) is indubitably in line with the particular way in which our psalm uses the name Zion. A fourth similarity! The Sons of Zion thus addressed should, according to Joel 2.21, 23, 'rejoice, that great things are done to them! This rejoicing is expressed in Ps. 126.3 by the same root in an exactly similar way. A fifth connection! Especially noteworthy are Joel 3 verses 1,2,4. The promise given here says that as a sign of the salvation to come, the approaching day of the Lord, God's people will dream like prophets (22) and see visions. (23) Doesn't this Joel promise correspond with what 126.1 presupposes? Doesn't this promise resolve the problem of this disputed, difficult psalm text? That just before the restoration all the Lord's people should dream dreams usually reserved to prophets! Or more precisely that all should be in a state corresponding to such a dream. Doesn't our psalm show the sign of the Lord's day, in which Zion will finally be restored, as already existing in the present, that now they are, at the moment of the psalm's reciting, in the preparatory stage for the definitive arrival of salvation? What we saw in chapters 2 and 3, long before we made the comparison with Joel, should now be recalled: Zion's restoration, Ps. 126.1a, is in all probability still in

---

[20] There is nothing even approximately similar. See S. Mandelkern, *Veteris Testamenti Concordantiae,* I., 2512.

[21] Cf. eg. 21.23; 24.12, 14; 26.29; Jos. 2.12; Judges 5.20; 8.35; 1 Sam. 16.5-2 Sam. 2.6-10.2; Kings 3.6.; Pss. 119.65, 124; Job 42.8; Ruth 1.8.

[22] Cf. on the one hand Jer. 23. 25ff or Mic. 3.5ff. and on the other, A.R. Johnson op.cit., 31-37.

[23] For the interpretation of this Joel passage see A.S. Kapelrud, op.cit., 127ff and especially W. Rudolph, KAT XIII 2, 71f.

the future. On the other hand the condition of being 'like dreamers' Ps. 126.1b, in accordance with its use of the Perfect *hajînû,* is already fully present! This present state (of being like dreamers) is therefore, according to all the rules of logic, previous to the eschatological restoration, is a 'sign' of it, the preparatory stage in which people — just as in prophetic dreams — (24) see in anticipation the final stage soon to come. In fact, what we showed to be the meaning of this psalm verse before we made the comparison with Joel, corresponds to the expectations described in Joel 3.1, 2, 4. To continue with our counting of similarities, this is the sixth! And this is still not all: for Joel too expresses what the Lord will do to save his people on that day by the term *sûb sᵉbût* (Joel 4.1). A seventh very important connection is the comparison with Ps. 126.1,4. The prophet also expects that all the Jewish water courses (ᵒ kol'ᵃphîkê jᵉhûda) will no longer be dried up 'on that day', the day of restoration, but that they too will be restored and carry water again (Joel 4.18; contrast Joel 1.20). Does not the community of Zion pray that their own restoration should go together with that of the water courses in nature, for restoration for both? 'Restore our fortunes, O Lord, like the water-courses in the Negeb.' 126.4 Isn't there a comparison here with the suddenness with which the water courses of Judah changed into rushing streams? (25) Isn't there also a reference here to the fact that eschatological restoration will affect both history and nature? If we answer this question in the affirmative — and I think we must — (26) then we have here a further correspondence between Joel's prophecy and our psalm; this would be the eighth. Finally we should note that in Joel's view the idea of *sûb sᵉbût* is

---

[24] Cf. again W. Rudolph, op.cit., 72.

[25] Cf. Y. Aharoni, op.cit., p.24 or O. Keel, *Die Welt der altorientalischen Bildsymbolik,* 63, 209.

[26] The expectation of salvation incorporating 'nature' and extending beyond the domain of history is quite a favourite subject. Cf (with Joel 4.17-18) esp. Is. 10.33-11.9; Hos.2.18-25; Am. 9.11-15; Is. 41.17-20; 43.16-22; Pss.85.9-14.

linked with the expectation of harvest, the object of which are the nations now ripe for judgement (cf. esp. Joel 4.13). Of course the psalm poem does not make plain what the harvest is to be (126.5,6). However it is not accidental that what it hopes for and expects is thought of as a 'harvest'. This would then be the ninth link in the already long chain of correspondences between Joel's prophecy and the psalm. Finally we should not overlook the fact that the prophet, before he promises the eschatological harvest, calls for conversion, fasting and weeping (Joel 2.12). We may well ask whether the contrast between weeping and reaping given us by our psalm (126.5,6) is not another connection between the two texts. Whether we are inclined to agree with this and make a tenth connection, or whether we decide to leave this last point open, (27) one way or the other, there are many certain points of contact which lead to the firm conclusion that Psalm 126 is closely related to the prophecy of Joel. The nature of this relationship will be determined more closely in what follows, especially the questions about the placement of the psalm, which need further clarification.

5.5. First a word about the *temporal* relationship between the two texts. Our findings on its historical context (28) showed us — before we made the comparison with Joel and therfore independently from this comparison! — that Psalm 126 was composed during the exile, neither earlier nor later. Here we put this result to use. There is no common opinion on the dating of Joel's prophecy. We think that the view put forward by Kapelrud and Rudolph has most in its favour: none of the arguments (29)

---

[27] Not least because the connection between weeping and reaping derives from much further back, from the ancient view of sowing as a time of sadness. Cf.A. Weiser, op.cit., 526 and M.P. Nilsson, *Geschichte der griechischen Religion,* 639. (The one derivation does not automatically exclude the other).

[28] See above chapter 4, esp. 4.5.

[29] Cf. A.S. Kapelrud, op.cit., esp. 181-192 and W. Rudolph, KAT CIII 2, 23-92, esp. 25-28.

for a post-exilic date stand up to close investigation. The most likely period for the composition of Joel is that between 597 and 587 B.C. (30) In this case the Joel prophecy would be earlier than our psalm. Joel would have been composed just before the exilic period and Psalm 126 during it. Thus the relationship between the two texts would depend on our Psalm presupposing the witness of the prophet Joel and not vice versa.

Now as we have said, the dating of Joel is disputed. It is therefore advisable to attempt a counter-proof. The assumption that Joel's prophecy came before the psalm poem means that this or that element of our psalm must be seen as a development of Joel's thought and not as a forerunner to it. In fact we can prove this in at least one point of contact. For if we make a more exact comparison between the way *dreaming* is spoken of in each text, there can be no doubt as to where the concept is simpler and where more developed, where it is more original and where it is modified. Joel 3.1, promises that all God's people will dream 'before the day of the Lord comes'. (31) Psalm 126 also speaks of dreaming but as if this period preliminary to the day of the Lord had already arrived. Of course it does not say so straight out but suggests this by the comparison. The speakers in the psalm are already in the preliminary stage to the day of the Lord, the day of eschatological restoration; they do not really dream but are *like* dreamers. What Joel promised, has according to the psalmist been fulfilled, differently from the way in which the prophet expected, but with the same result: insofar as the members of the community of Zion anticipate the future like prophetic dreamers. (32) They are *keholemîm* 'like dreamers'.

I think it is quite clear that Joel's promise does not develop the thought in the psalm, but is the prophetic forerunner to it. The psalmist sees the time prophesied by Joel as having arrived, the

---

[30] See W. Rudolph, op.cit., esp. 26. (For Joel 4.4.-8. see op.cit., 80-82.) Very similarly, A.S. Kapelrud, op.cit., esp. 191.

[31] See 4b.

[32] Cf. W. Rudolph, op.cit. 72.

preliminary stage to the day of the Lord as already come. Thus he modifies Joel's promise. Therefore the psalm is later than Joel. Or to put it differently: Joel's prophecy precedes the psalm in time. If we accept that the psalm dates from the exilic period, this harmonises with the view that Joel operated in the years immediately before the exile. This counter proof therefore supports the view of Kapelrud and Rudolph. But above all it strengthens our impression that Joel's prophecy already existed for our psalmist.

5.6. In what way did it already exist for him? If Psalm 126 was merely similar to Joel in substance, and not in the choice of words, then we could not exclude the possibility that the psalmist did not have Joel's text to hand but simply knew of it. It would also be possible that the psalmist composed from within the same tradition in which Joel ben Petuel stood. Then the relationship as shown by the similarities in the two texts would be a matter of derivation from the same tradition. However Psalm 126 is not merely similar in thoughts to Joel but there are actual verbal similarities. This is particularly the case with 126.2b. This line of poem follows the Joel text verbatim. (33) *jo'merû be* corresponds to Joel 2.17, *baggôjim* to Joel 2.19, *higdîl jhwh la ca' sôt* to Joel 2.21, *caśa cim* to Joel 2.26. The psalmist uses these expressions in exactly the same order as Joel. This means that he must have had to hand the words of Joel in written form. There is nothing against this assumption. For the opinion expressed by Kapelrud that it was probably only late, in the fourth or third centuries, that Joel's words were written down, (34) can in no way be proved. (35) Of course this does not mean that our psalm was composed merely by scholarly borrowing, but it does mean that it was influenced by the Joel tradition in *written* form. The tradition on which the psalmist principally relied is quite clear.

---

[33] Apart from its beginning and end.

[34] Cf. op.cit., p. 180, 192.

[35] As A.S. Kapelrud says quite clearly himself (op.cit., p. 192). The author shares W. Rudolph's scepticism here (op.cit., p. 24).

5.7. This brings us back to a question we mentioned before: whence did our psalm derive? (36) Once we establish *where* Joel's prophecy was handed down, we establish *eo ipso* where the use of this prophetic tradition was a real possibility. One thing is certain, namely that Joel worked in Jerusalem. This it is almost certain that his words were noted and handed down in Jerusalem and perhaps in surrounding Judah. It is much less probable that they were handed down in a parallel manner also in Gola. This means that the author of our psalm, who as we have seen was influenced by the Joel tradition in written form, (37) is more likely to have lived in Jerusalem-Judah than in exile in Babylon. This means that we explain Ps. 126.4b's reference to the water courses of the Negeb as a local reference, not one made from abroad. (38) The psalmist is talking about something within his own experience. Thus we can say: the proof is not watertight but the probabilities are heavily in favour of Psalm 126 having been composed in Jerusalem-Judah. (39)

5.8. If, as we have shown, (40) our psalm is based on the proclamation of the prophet Joel, this also tells us something else about its tradition: the psalmist must have been at home within the *prophetic* tradition. There were already signs of this in previous investigations we made: the elements of the psalm we discussed — before we made the comparison with Joel's words — were mostly, if not exclusively, used in prophetic contexts. (41) This already led us to think that our psalm also derived from prophetic sources. Then our demonstration of the special close relationships between the psalm and the prophecy of Joel makes this a certainty: Psalm

---

[36] This question was mentioned in 5.2. and 5.3.

[37] See above chap. 5.6.

[38] See above chap. 5.3.

[39] See also the last note in chap. 5.9. (note 60).

[40] Cf. chap. 5.4. and 5.6.

[41] See above, esp. chap. 5.1.

126 arose from the prophetic tradition. But this is not all. The point in the history of tradition at which our psalm arose can be determined more closely. For Joel ben Petuel counts among the *prophets of salvation*. To put it more precisely, when he spoke the words that have come down to us, he changed from a prophet of doom to a prophet of salvation. (42) The elements of Joel's prophecy that our psalmist assimilated were all of the salvation prophecy type. No wonder this was what he latched onto! This prophecy of salvation suited the psalmist's intentions. For he too was concerned with Zion's salvation. According to him this was so close, that it could not only be prayed for but also anticipated. Reference to a corresponding prophecy of salvation was in accordance with what he wanted to say. This shows the point in the history of tradition at which our psalm arose.

5.9. Finally, it remains to ask, where and in what way did the psalmist go beyond his tradition? Compared with Joel's prophecies, what did he see differently? We can only set the psalm firmly in the history of tradition when we have discovered this, and thus established its co-ordinates.

The dates we have given caused the obvious changes: if we date Joel before 587, the year of catastrophe for the Southern Kingdom, and Psalm 126, after that date, during the exilic period, then we have placed the catastrophe between the two texts, an historical caesura, which must have caused changes.

The *first* change was that Joel's conviction that Jerusalem would be untouched, that the Lord's people would never again come to grief, (43) was destroyed by the catastrophe. When the psalmist takes up the prophetic expectation of a final restoration of Zion (44) this is not just repetition. He is saying something new, making a new act of faith. This faith is aware of the changed conditions, the enduring need, suffering and tears. (Ps. 126. 5,6).

---

[42] Cf. W. Rudolph, op.cit., esp. 88-91

[43] Cf. Chaps. 3 and 4.

[44] Joel 4.1.

A faith which sees these tears as seed, seed which brings forth the harvest. The constant weeping is the reason why the Lord will do great things and finally restore Zion, which is a different viewpoint from that in Joel's time. This weeping during the exile is the cause of the hope which Joel — who still did not know of this reason and was thus in advance of the times — spoke about. The experience of suffering during the exile deepens the expectation spoken of by Joel: 'They who sow in tears will reap with joy' (v.5.) Tears and suffering are an integral part of the process which will bring about Zion's restoration. (45) Perhaps we might want to say that there was already a certain polarity between weeping and reaping in Joel. In fact this is true, as we have seen earlier. (46) However the weeping in Joel 2.12 is not as deep as that in the psalm. In Joel the weeping is of the cultic ritual kind. (47) This may also be true of the psalmist but he is not only this. He chiefly gives the impression of constant deep suffering. (48) If the psalmist was in fact also influenced by Joel here (we left the question open) it would still be true that his conception of weeping and reaping would be quite different — his expectation of salvation would be more pressing. At any rate weeping and suffering have their place in the psalm's expectation of salvation. They are in the context of a process which will end with God restoring all things. (49) A *second change* cannot be fully proved. But it is apparent in the difference between the two texts on the

---

45 It is possible that in this thought in the psalm we have a proverb, an element of traditional wisdom.

46 See above chap. 5.4.

47 Cf. W. Rudolph, op.cit., 58. See also F. Hvidberg, *Vom Weinen und Lachen im AT.* In this context it is also worth mentioning that Joel was a cult prophet. See A.S. Kapelrud, op.cit., esp. 176f., 185f.; W. Rudolph, op.cit., esp. 25f. (Fundamental are S. Mowinckel, *Psalmenstudien III* and A.R. Johnson, op.cit. Further bibliography in W. Rudolph, op.cit., 25).

48 The image of the sower weeping up and down furrow after furrow (Ps. 126.6) gives this impression, I think. Cf. also A. Weiser, op.cit., 526.

49 This also gave a new interpretation of suffering.

point of the scope of the eschatological restoration. The prophecy of Joel makes plain that the restoration will also include 'nature' (cf. esp. Joel 4.18). The psalm poem only speaks of this, if at all, by implication (Ps. 126.4b). (50) Does this mean that the author of the psalm, because of the misery of the exile, concentrated *more* than Joel on restoration in the historical sphere? (51) We cannot be sure of this, because we should remember that the psalmist was constrained by his form: he was writing a poem. But within this framework, perhaps it is important that the water courses of the Negeb are mentioned. Moreover for an ancient Israelite who understood the language of tradition the reference in verse 4b may have expressed, as *pars pro toto,* far more than at first appears to us. This is the best basis for the question whether the psalmist's emphasis in the scope of restoration was different from Joel's. In a third respect the author of the psalm in fact thought differently from Joel: about the nations, the Gentiles. In the view of the *prophets* the restoration of the Lord's own people had an opposite side: when the Lord restored his people he would destroy all the *gôjim.* Metaphorically they were ripe for harvest, literally they were ripe for God's judgement and vengeance (Joel 4.1 - 21). (52). The psalm is quite different in this respect. It does use the image of the harvest but not threateningly about the outsiders; it refers to the salvation of the community itself (126.5,6): the harvest is Zion's fulfilment, its restoration. There is no mention of an opposite side, there is no suggestion that salvation for the Lord's community means *eo ipso* destruction of the *gôjim.* This is an arguement from silence. But it stands, because the psalmist does speak expressly about the nations. He mentions them in 126.2b with reference to Jaweh's saving action. Of course the *gôjim* are not the objects of this salvation. However they see and recognise it and speak of it with praise: (53) 'When the Lord restored the

---

[50] This is presupposed in the detailed interpretation of the text in chap. 5.4.

[51] This division into 'spheres' is in any case merely an inadequate working aid.

[52] 4. 4-8 is an interpolation.

[53] Compare half verse 2b with the praise uttered by the Zion community in V3a.

fortunes of Zion, then they said among the nations: The Lord has done great things for them.' The psalmist is interested in the silencing of the nations' mockery and their recognition of the Lord's action for his people. In this way the author of the psalm shows himself, as we saw earlier, (54) to be a child of his time, a child of the exilic period. He is outstanding in that his formulation is not aggressive. If we go by the psalm text, he has no place for thoughts about a judgment of the nations. In an impressive way he concentrates on the inner aspect of misery. What he is interested in — to repeat once more — is that the *restitutio in integrum* includes the removal of the thorn represented by the nations' mockery, that the nations' should recognise Zion's restoration and the wound caused by this thorn be healed. All in all, it is clear that the psalmist who was so strongly influenced by Joel's prophecy, has a less aggressive viewpoint here than Joel's. His expectation of salvation does not stretch to salvation for all. But he is far removed the nationalistic and particularistic conception of Joel. He does not expect the Lord to deal with nations vengefully as Joel does; for him they are ready to acknowledge the greatness of the Lord's action. A *fourth* difference from Joel's way of thinking has already been mentioned: (55) The psalmist takes the theme that all God's people will dream in the preliminary stage to the day of the Lord (56) and changes it. The early sign of the restoration has been fulfilled in a different way from Joel's prophecy. In Zion the people do not really dream. The members of God's community do not see what the Lord is about to do by means of charismatic and prophetic dreams. And yet they foresee in the certainty of their faith, and thus are like dreamers. Because this anticipatory certainty of faith is present reality, because the members of the community of Zion are like dreamers, the early sign of the Lord's day has arrived, Zion's restoration is at

---

[54] See above chap. 4.5.

[55] See above chap. 5.5.

[56] Joel 3. 1,4.

hand. In this thought we see a *fifth* difference in the psalmist's thinking from Joel's: compared with Joel, for him the time is dramatically foreshortened. Zion's restoration is very near. Its preliminary stage has come: the phase of its early warning sign is present. During the sufferings of the exile, there arose a faith which saw the Lord's restoring salvation as much more immanent than Joel thought.

The psalm's certainty of the nearness of salvation is great, so great that the failure of the early sign to be fulfilled literally, the fact that prophetic dreams have not become common throughout the population, does not matter. It does not matter because Joel's expectation has been fulfilled in essentials. The faith of the community of Zion is just as good as prophetic dreaming, (57) the foreseeing of what the Lord will shortly bring to pass. The psalmist is quite certain the anticipatory faith of the community is like prophetic dreaming: *hajînû k^ehol^emîm:* 'We are — fully and truly — *like* dreamers. (58) This sign conceived by the prophet in a specifically prophetic way is transformed in the community psalm into a communal experience. The author of the psalm writes from the prophetic tradition, but is not confined within it. He goes further and says what is possible and viable for the community, for non-prophets. (59).

---

[57] Cf. W. Rudolph, op.cit., 72.

[58] Note the perfect hajînû.

[59] Another marginal note. Perhaps the transformation process here was that which was already visible in Ps. 74.9 and Lam. 2.9. In the Jerusalem region during the exile, whence the above texts as well as our psalm arose, apparently there had not been (cult) prophetic revelations for a long while. Cf. H.-J. Kraus, BK XV/1, 517; BK XX, 40. If we go by these texts, we find the opposite to that which Joel, the prophet of salvation had foretold before the exile. The charisma of prophetic foresight did not become common to all. It was in fact (at any rate in the Jerusalem region) altogether lost. Possibly the author of Ps. 126 reached his position because of these circumstances. This would accord best with our view. Otherwise this historical circumstance, if it were really the background to our text, could upset our timing and placing of Cf. above chap. 4.5; 5.3 and 5.7.

Conclusion

In conclusion we can say:

6.1. Our disentangling of the problems followed this order:
a) we tried to understand the comparison with dreamers uninfluenced by linguistic modernisms in an ancient Israelite way and
b) we investigated the context in history and tradition of the psalm. Our analysis of the linguistic form supported our thesis.

6.2 The Lord's community in South Palestine ('Zion') who are behind the psalm compares itself to dreamers, because they anticipate in faith what God is going to do, and they experience in advance what — God willing — the future will bring. Because of this anticipatory experience, the community is filled with joy in the present and ready to praise the Lord. But because their *restitutio in integrum* is not yet manifest in normal everyday experience, they are at the same time suffering and weeping. (1)

6.3. The tension between the two halves of the psalm which has caused so much confusion, is not, as is usually thought, due to two different historical situations. It is a tension within the same situation. It is the often experienced and easily understood tension between the salvation already apprehended in faith and the plea that it might 'appear'.

6.4. The salvation which is already real but still hidden in God, does leave some scope for the human will. There is room for communal human prayer, that this salvation should become fully manifest. (2)

---

[1] See above, esp. chap. 2.6.

[2] See chap. 2. note 35.

6.5. The two-part nature of our psalm is reflected in its changes of rhythm and style. (3)

6.6. Our interpretation of the text is thus supported by its grammar and syntax. (4)

6.7. Essentially it is community of the Lord which looks forward to the certainty of faith. For this very reason its psalm is totally unliturgical. On the other hand it is neither a hymn nor a people's lament. Because it anticipates coming salvation in the boldness of faith and also prays for it, it is partly a making present of salvation and partly a prayer of petition. It therefore expresses trust in the certainty of imminent salvation made present. (5)

6.8. Its context in life is almost certainly the communal cult, or more precisely, the cult of the Zion community. There is not the slightest textual support for seriously upholding a more specialised place for it. (6)

6.9. The psalm's historical context — especially when we consider its concern with what the nations say — (7) is the situation of the exilic period, apparently at home in South Palestine.(8) There is no doubt at all that this situation (not just this one, but this as well as another) could be felt to be a time of wearisome sowing in tears. At any rate the individual details of the text — separately and together! — permit the historical contextualisation which our research into the themes of the psalm, taken as a whole, require.(9)

---

[3] See above chap. 3.1. and 3.2.

[4] See above chap. 3.3.

[5] See above chap. 3.4.

[6] See above chap. 3.4. See also chap. 1, note 41.

[7] See above chap. 4.5. and also 4.3. and 4.4.

[8] See above chap. 5.2. - 5.3, esp. 5.7.

[9] Above all, as we have said the research in chap. 4.5.

6.10. As the analysis of its themes showed (10) the content of the poem is drawn principally (11) from prophetic sources. When we have made the comparison with Joel's words, we find its special connection with him. The psalmist refers constantly to the prophecy of Joel ben Petuel, and apparently had it to hand in a literary form. (12) The psalm's starting point in the history of tradition is thus Joel's prophecy of salvation and with it, in part, a developed tradition of Zion. (13)

6.11. Joel's beliefs — like those of many others! — were shaken by the catastrophe of 587 and became more than questionable. Reaffirmation of them, a renewal of the expectation of a definitive restoration of Zion was therefore an act of faith. An act of faith which had learnt from history. (14) The experience of suffering during the exile deepened the expectation of salvation and included the idea that without the seed of tears there could be no harvest. It brought the faith that this sowing, which seemed to take so long brought the harvest nearer. The community of the psalm feels itself, unlike Joel, to be already in the preliminary stage to the day of the Lord. The fact that they do not have the early sign of this day, universal prophetic dreaming, does not bother them: the sign is present by their anticipating in faith, which makes them like prophetic dreamers. The early sign that the prophet conceived of in a manner suited to his own condition is fulfilled, in the present, in the community, in a manner transformed to suit the community means, the day of the Lord is at hand and finally about to break. Other signs of prophetic expectation of salvation, like the changing of the moon into blood

---

[10] See as well as chap. 4.3. - 4.5. esp. 5.1.

[11] However cf. the summary of contrary opinion chap. 5, note 46.

[12] See above chap. 5.4. - 5.6.

[13] See chap. 5.8.

[14] Cf. chap. 5.9.

E

(15) do not come within the scope of the psalm. Neither does the expectation of the judgment of the nations. In the psalm the restoration of Zion loses its aggressive opposite side which it had in Joel. The experience of suffering during the exile apparently taught the people to hate less rather than more, made them more mature, not least because they now feel it was enough if the contempt of the Gentiles was eliminated and not the Gentiles themselves too. Yes, it is more than enough if the *gôjim,* instead of mocking as before, recognise the Lord's action for the salvation of his people, recognise it in words of praise. The psalm refrains from saying what will become of the nations now that they have offered this recognition. This appears to be a broader view than selfish concern only for nationalistic salvation.

6.12. A highly significant poem! Once we have correctly understood the comparison with dreamers, its difficulties are overcome surprisingly easily. Psalm 126 is the witness of a yearning expectant faith, sure of salvation to come, a faith which has matured through suffering and learnt that tears are seed and those who endure will reap their harvest. The poem is full of movement. It takes up the theme of eager expectation, develops it, includes suffering as part of the process of final salvation, changes the specifically prophetic into the communal and strives to go beyond a narrow nationalistic concept of salvation. We cannot dispute the exceptional beauty of its poetic form, it has often been noted and needs no further discussion. We can only agree with Duhm's praise quoted at the beginning of this work: Psalm 126 is one of the most beautiful poems, if not the most beautiful in the whole psalter, both in content and form. It is a mature, profound and moving witness to patient and certain faith. We hope that this study has helped to make clearer the reasons for this high praise.

---

[15] Cf. Joel 3.4.

Appendix

The Psalm 126 in the RSV English translation

V. 1a   When the Lord restored the fortunes of Zion,

V. 1b   —we are like those who dream —

V. 2a   Then our mouth was filled with laughter, and our tongue with shouts of joy;

V. 2b   then they said among the nations, 'The Lord has done great things for them.'

V. 3a   The Lord has done great things for us;

V. 3b   we are glad.

V. 4a   Restore our fortunes, O Lord,

V. 4b   like the water courses in the Negeb!

V. 5a   May those who sow in tears

V. 5b   reap with shouts of joy!

V. 6a   He that goes forth weeping bearing the seed for sowing,

V. 6b   shall come home with shouts of joy, bringing his sheaves with him.

Abbreviations

Bibliography

Abaroni Y., The Land of the Bible. A Historical Geography, London, 2E, 1968.

Alonso-Schökel L., Das Alte Testament als literarisches Kunstwerk, Köln 1971.

Anderson A.A., The Book of Psalms, II (NCeB), London 1972.

Baethgen F., Die Psalmen (HK 11 2), Göttingen, 3E,1904.

Baumann E., sûb sᵉbût. Eine exegetische Untersuchung: ZAW 47 (1929) 17-44.

— Struktur-Untersuchungen im Psalter II: ZAW 62 (1950) 115-152.

Becker J., Israel deutet seine Psalmen. Urform und Neuinterpretation in den Psalmen (SBS 18), Stuttgart 1966.

Begrich J., Der Satzstil im Fünfer: ZS 9 (1934) 169-209, in: Gesammelte Studien zum Alten Testament (ThB 21), München 1964, 132-167.

Bernhardt K.-H., Ugaritische Texte, in: *W. Beyerlin* (Ed.), Religionsgeschichtliches Textbuch zum Alten Testament, Grundrisse zum Alten Testament (ATD Ergänzungsreihe 1), Göttingen 1975, 205-243.

Bertholet A., Das Buch der Psalmen (HSAT [K] Bd. 2), Tübingen, 4E, 1923

Beyerlin W., Die Reitung der Bedrängten in den Feindpsalmen der Einzelnen auf institutionelle Zusammenhänge untersucht (FRLANT 99), Göttingen 1970.

— (Ed.), Religionsgeschichtliches Textbuch zum Alten Testament, Grundrisse zum Alten Testament (ATD Ergänzungsreihe 1), Göttingen 1975.

— Innerbiblische Aktualisierungsversuche: Schichten im 44. Psalm: ZThK 73 (1976) 446-460.

Bonkamp B., Die Psalmen nach dem hebräischen Grundtext übersetzt, Freiburg 1949.

Borger R., Zu sûb sᵉbût/ît: ZAW 66 (1954) 315-316.

Briggs C.A. u. *E.G.,* A Critical and Exegetical Commentary on the Book of Psalms, II (ICC), Edinburgh 1960.

Brockleman C., Hebräische Syntax, Neukirchen 1956.

Büblmann W. Scherer K., Stilfiguren der Bibel (BiBe 10) Einsiedeln-Stuttgart 1973.

Buttenwieser M., The Psalms Chronologically Treated (1938), (LBS), New York, 2E, 1969.

Castellino G.R., Libro dei Salmi, Turin-Rom 1965.

Culley R. C., Oral Formulaic Language in the Biblical Psalms, Toronto 1967.

Dahood M., Psalms (AncB 17A), Garden City N.Y. 1970.

Deutsches Wörterbuch von *Jacob Grimm und Wilhelm Grimm,* edited by M. Lexer, D. Kralik und der Arbeitsstelle des Deutschen Wörterbuchs, 11. Bd., 1. Abt., 1. Teil, Leipzig 1935.

Dietrich E. L., sûb sᵉbût. Die endzeitliche Wiederherstellung bei den Propheten (BZAW 40), Gießen 1925.

Duhm B., Die Psalmen (KHC XIV), Freiburg-Leipzig-Tübingen, 2E, 1922.

Dupont-Sommer A. & J. Starky, Une inscription araméenne inédite de Sfiré (Bulletin du Musée de Beyrouth 13), Paris 1956, 23—41.

Ehrlich E. L., Der Traum im Alten Testament (BZAW 73), Berlin 1953.

— Traum, in: BHH III, Göttingen 1966, 2023 - 2025.

Elliger K., Leviticus (HAT I 4), Tübingen 1966.

Fitzmyer J.A., The Aramaic Inscriptions of Sefirê (BibOr 19), Rom 1967.

Fohrer G., Das Buch Hiob (KAT XVI), Gütersloh 1963.

Gemser B., Sprüche Salomos (HAT I 16), Tübingen, 2E, 1963.

Goldschmidt L., Der babylonische Talmud, III, Berlin, 2E, 1965.

Gunkel H., Die Psalmen (HK II 2), Göttingen, 4E, 1926.

Gunkel H.-Begrich J., Einleitung in die Psalmen, Göttingen, 2E, 1966.

Herkenne H., Das Buch der Psalmen (HSAT V 2), Bonn 1936.

Hupfeld H., Die Psalmen, IV, Gotha 1862.

Hvidberg F., Vom Weinen und Lachen im AT: ZAW 57 (1939) 150-152.

van Imschoot P., Traum, in: BL Einsiedeln 1781, 2E, 1964.

Johnson A.R., The Cultic Prophet in Ancient Israel, Cardiff, 2E, 1962.

Kaiser O., Der Prophet Jesaja Kapitel 13-39 (ATD 18), Göttingen 1973.

Kapelrud A.S., Joel Studies, Uppsala 1948.

Keel O., Die Welt der altorientalischen Bildsymbolik und das Alte Testament, Zürich-Einsiedeln-Köln-Neukirchen 1972.

Keet C.C., A study of the Psalms of Ascents. A Critical and Exegetical Commentary upon Psalms CXX to CXXXIV, London 1969.

Kirkpatrik A.F., The Book of Psalms, Cambridge 1906.

Kissane E.J., The Book of Psalms, Dublin 1964.

Kittel R., Die Psalmen (KAT XIII), Leipzig-Erlangen, 6E, 1929.

Kraus H.-J., Klagelieder (Threni) (BK XX), Neukirchen 1956.

— Psalmen, I.II (BK XV/1.2), Neukirchen 1960.

Lambert W.G., Babylonian Wisdom Literature, Oxford, 3E, 1975.

Langdon St., Babylonian Wisdom: Bab. 7 (1913-1923) 129-229.

Leslie E.A., The Psalms. Translated and Interpreted in the Light of Hebrew Life and Worship, Nashville N.Y. 1949.

Lipiński E., Nordsemitische Texte, in: *W. Beyerlin* (Ed.), Religionsgeschichtliches Textbuch zum Alten Testament, Grundrisse zum Alten Testament (ATD Ergänzungsreihe 1), Göttingen 1975, 245-284.

Mandelkern S., Veteris Testamenti Concordantiaé Hebraicae atque Chaldaicae, I.II Graz, 2E, 1955.

Mannati M., Les Psaumes, IV (Cahiers de la Pierre-qui-vire), Paris 1968.

Meyer R., Das Gebet des Nabonid. Eine in den Qumran-Handschriften wiederentdeckte Weischeitserzahlung (SSAW. PH 107/3) Berlin 1962

— Hebräische Grammatik, I (SG 763/763a/763b), Berlin 1966; III (SG 5765), Berlin 1972.

Michel D., Tempora und Satzstellung in den Psalmen, Diss. Bonn 1960.

Morgenstern J., Psalm 126, in: Homenaje a Millás-Vallicrosa, II, Barcelona 1956, 109-117.

Mowinckel S., Psalmenstudien III. Kultprophetie und prophetische Psalmen (1923), Neudruck Amsterdam 1961.

— The Psalms in Israel's Worship, II, Oxford 1962.

Nilsson M.P., Geschichte der griechischen Religion (HAW, V. Abt., II 1), München 1941.

Nötscher F., Die Psalmen (EB), Würzburg 1959.

Oesterley W.O.E., The Psalms, London 1959.

Olshausen J., Die Psalmen (KEH), Leipzig 1853.

Oppenheim A.L., The Interpretation of Dreams in the Ancient Near East, in: Transactions of the American Philosophical Society (NS Bd. 46, Vol. 3), Philadelphia 1956, 179-373.

The Oxford English Dictionary, See also the New English Dictionary on Historical Principles, edited by *J.A.H. Murray, H. Bradley et.al.* III, Oxford 1933.

Pedersen J., Israel. Its Life and Culture, I.II., London 1926.

Porteous N.W., Jerusalem — Zion: The Growth of a Symbol in: Verbannung und Heimkehr, Festschrift f. W. Rudolph, Tübingen 1961, 235-252, reproduced as: Living the Mystery, Oxford 1967, 93-111.

Resch A., Der Traum im Heilsplan Gottes. Deutung und Bedeutung des Traums im Alten Testament, Freiburg-Basel-Wien 1964.

Robinson H. Wheeler, The Hebrew Conception of Corporate Personality, in: Werden und Wesen des Alten Testaments (BZAW 66), Berlin 1936, 49-62.

Routley E., Exploring the Psalms, Philadelphia 1975.

Rudolph W., Jeremia (HAT I 12), Tübingen, 2E, 1958.

— Hosea (KAT XIII 1), Gütersloh 1966.

— Joel-Amos-Obadja-Jona (KAT XIII 2), Gütersloh 1971.

Sanders J.A., The Psalms Scroll of Qumrân Cave 11 (DJD IV), Oxford 1965.

Schmidt H., Die Psalmen (HAT I 15), Tübingen 1934.

Schmidtke F., Träume, Orakel und Totengeister als Künder der Zukunft in Israel und Babylonien: BZ NF 11 (1967) 240-246.

Segert S., Einige Bemerkungen zur akkadischen Lexikographie: Archiv Orientální 32 (1964) 127-131.

v. Soden W., Akkadisches Handwörterbuch, III, Wiesbaden 1974 ff.

Staerk W., Lyrik (SAT 3. Abt. 1. Bd), Göttingen, 2E, 1920.

Stolz F., Sijjon Zion, in: THAT II (1976), 543-551.

Strugnell J., A Note on Ps. CXXVI.1: JThSt NS 7 (1956) 239-243.

Weber J.J., Le Psautier, Paris, 2E, 1968.

Weiser A., Die Psalmen (ATD 14/15), Göttingen, 8E, 1973.

de Wette W.M.L., Commentar über die Psalmen, Heidelberg, 5E, 1856.

Wolff H.W., Dodekapropheton 1, Hosea (BK XIV/1), Neukirchen, 2E, 1965.

Wünsche A., Midrasch Tehillim oder haggadische Erklärung der Psalmen, II (1893), Nachdruck Hildesheim 1967.

Zimmerli W., Ezechiel, I.II (BK XIII/1.2), Neukirchen 1969.

Zimmern H., Babylonische Busspsalmen, Leipzig 1885.

List of Biblical References

(Raised figures = in Footnotes)
(Figures in brackets = quoted in text and footnotes)

Gen
2,4b—7 36[16]
20,3ff 25.28
21,23 54[22]
24,12.14 54[22]
26,29 54[22]
28,16 25
31,24 25
37ff 28.29
41,1—7 29
41,7 25
41,28 29
42,9.11.31 35

Lev
26,45 48[29]

Num
12,6 28
12,6—8 26

Dtn
28,36.37 47
29,23 47
30,3 43.51[1]

Jos
2,12 54[22]

Judg
5,20 54[22]
7 29
7,9ff.13ff 29
7,13.14 28
8,35 54[22]

1 Sam
11,2 46[20]
16,5 54[22]
17,26 46[20]

2 Sam
2,6 54[22]
10,2 54[22]

1 Kings
3,5ff 28
3,6 54[22]
3,15 25
9,7 47

Isq
1,8 45[17]
10,33—11,9 56[27]
29,7.8 26.27
41,17—20 56[27]
42,8 48[30].52[9].
    53[16]
43,16—21 56[27]
48,1.2 45.51[4].
    52[14]
48,11 48[30].52[9].
    53[16]
49,14ff 45.51[4].52[14]
15,11 42
52,1ff 45.51[4].52[14]
52,10 48.49[33].
    52[9].53[16]

Jer
23,23—32 28[24].55[23]
24,9 46
27,9—10 28[24]
29,8—9 28[24]
29,14 43.51[3].52[10]
30,3.18 43.51[3]52[10]
31,23 43.51[3].52[10]
32,44 43[10].51[3]
33,7 44
33,7.11 52[10]
33,7.11.26 51[3]
33,11 43
33,26 43[10]